A FLAME OF SACRED LOVE

A FLAME OF SACRED LOVE

The Life of Benjamin Broomhall
1829–1911

By Norman Cliff

OM
publishing

First published in 1998 by OM Publishing

04 03 02 01 00 99 98   7 6 5 4 3 2 1

OM Publishing is an imprint of Paternoster Publishing,
P.O. Box 300, Carlisle, Cumbria, CA3 OQS, U.K.
http://www.paternoster-publishing.com

British Library Cataloguing in Publication Data
A catalogue record for this book is available from the British Library.

ISBN 1-85078-328-4

Cover design by Mainstream, Lancaster
Typeset by WestKey Ltd, Falmouth, Cornwall
Printed in Great Britain by Mackays of Chatham PLC, Kent

O Thou, who camest from above,
  The pure, celestial fire to impart,
Kindle a flame of sacred love
  On the mean altar of my heart.

Charles Wesley.

This book is dedicated to

Gertrude Hoste
Hudson Broomhall
Edith Ritchie
Marshall Broomhall
Benjamin Broomhall

five children of Benjamin and Amelia Broomhall,
who, by faith, went to China as missionaries

Benjamin Broomhall, staunch advocate of missions and crusader against injustice.

Contents

Key to Abbreviations

BMS   Baptist Missionary Society
CIM   China Inland Mission
CMS   Church Missionary Society
IVF   Inter-Varsity Fellowship
MSI   Medical Services International
SCM   Student Christian Movement
SVM   Student Volunteer Movement
SVMU Student Volunteer Missionary Union
YMCA Young Men's Christian Association

The spelling of Chinese words, places and names

In general Chinese words have been spelt according to the present Pinyin system of transliteration.

Exceptions to this are:

i When a Chinese word is used in a quotation the original spelling has been retained, followed by the Pinyin spelling in square brackets.

ii Peking has not been changed as it is still well known under its old name.

iii Pastor Hsi Sheng Mo is referred to by the old Wade-Giles system of spelling, which is the spelling familiar to Westerners.

Foreword

Many Christians of my generation benefited greatly from reading the writings of Marshall Broomhall. Some of us were privileged to have known Paul Broomhall, who was actively involved in the work of the Bible and Medical Missionary Fellowship, as it was then known. With the publication of Dr. Norman Cliff's book we learn a great deal more about the involvement of the Broomhall family in overseas missions.

We are told of the missionary zeal of Benjamin Broomhall, a Christian layman who a century ago was urging Christians to become involved in evangelizing China, and who worked for 20 years at the headquarters of the China Inland Mission in London. When Benjamin joined the staff in 1875 there were 38 members, and when he retired 20 years later there were 630.

The writer of this fascinating volume is the great-grandson of Benjamin Broomhall, and he gives us some precious insights into the family's history. The book is also valuable as an account of an age of great scientific advance, coinciding with a period of phenomenal missionary expansion. It is a very readable story, providing a useful supplement to earlier accounts both of the life of Hudson Taylor and of the early years of the China Inland Mission.

I echo the author's words — 'May this biography be an inspiration to all who read it.'

(Rev.) Gilbert W. Kirby
General Secretary, Evangelical Alliance, 1957–1966

Introduction

Benjamin Broomhall was one of the best known Christian laymen in Britain in the latter part of the nineteenth century. He was known in churches of many denominations, where he either spoke on China himself or introduced returning missionaries as speakers. He attended and took part in the large conventions of that period, and pleaded cause of missions. He addressed the annual conferences of various Free Churches urging the delegates to commence missionary work in China. Cabinet ministers and members of Parliament knew him for his uncompromising stand on the questions of slavery and the opium trade.

Undoubtedly his greatest work was in the service of the China Inland Mission. Benjamin worked for 20 years at the mission's headquarters in Newington Green, north London, 18 of them as its General Secretary. This period has been described as the golden age of the mission. When Benjamin joined in 1875 there were 38 members, and when he retired 20 years later at the age of sixty-six, 630. Also, in addition to the inter-connecting houses in Pyrland Road, a four-storeyed building in Newington Green had been built.

Although he never set foot in China, his influence on God's work in that land was considerable. He interviewed, selected and sent out several hundred young men and women to work as missionaries there. As the Editor of *China's Millions* he acquired an intimate knowledge of the culture, customs and spiritual needs of that vast land, so that his articles and reports gave the Christian public the widest possible overview of the work.

The work of Amelia, his wife, though less prominent, was no less important. She was a mother figure to the young applicants who came to reside at Pyrland Road, and her love and encouragement at the time of their taking the very brave plunge of going to the little-known land of China, helped them in a way which they never forgot. She was a woman of prayer, and her life was one of constant love and care for others.

Dr. James Hudson Taylor, a friend of Benjamin's since they were young men together in Barnsley, and brother of Amelia, leaned very heavily on this dedicated couple through the difficult years of this period. He could never have carried out his remarkable programme of growth and extension in inland China without the loyalty and support of Benjamin and Amelia, and without the sound administrative base in London which they had made to back up his fast-growing work.

To write on the life work of my great-grandparents has been a tremendous privilege. I am greatly indebted to Marshall Broomhall, their son, for the brief biography which he wrote in 1918 under the title *Heirs Together of the Grace of Life*; also to Dr. A.J. Broomhall, their grandson, for the remarkable seven-volume history which he wrote under the general title of *Hudson Taylor and China's Open Century*, completed in 1989. I have also drawn valuable information from the mission's magazine, *China's Millions*. Other sources I have acknowledged in the Bibliography at the back of this book. Only for major quotations have I given chapter and verse at the end of a chapter.

I have been given help on the lives of the children and grandchildren of Benjamin Broomhall by Mrs. Thea Cunningham, Mrs. Maud MacCormac, Mrs. Alice Forrest, Mrs. Joy Lankester, Mrs. Josephine Wakeling, Mr. Findlay Dunachie and the Rev. Walter Ritchie — all descendants of Benjamin and Amelia. Mr. Geoffrey Palmer has put the early records of the YMCA at my disposal. The Rev. John Pollock has helped me with the story of the 'Cambridge Seven'. For any errors in the story I am solely responsible.

Books and documents have been made available to me at the following libraries and archival centres:

Anti-Slavery International, London
British Library, London
CMS Archives, Partnership House, London
Evangelical Alliance, London
Evangelical Library, London
Friends House, London
Guild Hall Library, London
Regent's Park College (BMS), Oxford
School of Oriental & African Studies, London

My wife, Joyce, has given me wonderful support and encouragement in researching the life of my great-grandfather, and has carefully checked the manuscript and made valuable suggestions. My son, James, has willingly helped with problems on the computer.

May this biography be an inspiration to all who read it.

1

Living in exciting times

There is no question about it. Benjamin Broomhall lived in exciting times. When he was nine years old Queen Victoria came to the throne, and she died when he was seventy-two and six years into retirement.

The long reign of this successful monarch saw the rise of Britain to the zenith of its power as 'the workshop of the world', the undisputed ruler of the seas and proud possessor of an empire embracing one quarter of the area of the world, and with its influence on every continent. And every decade of this reign brought further advances and discoveries.

But in spite of all these achievements, there was still in Britain shocking inequality and scandalous poverty, as described in the novels of Charles Dickens. In 1845 the Tory leader, Benjamin Disraeli, spoke of 'the two nations' — of the rich and the poor — who lived side by side in respectable Britain. Benjamin Broomhall, as a Methodist local preacher, was to see this side of the nation's life, as he visited people in the slums of East London. A man who wished to see a moral and just society, he performed many acts of kindness among the poor in this area, as well as witnessing to his faith in Christ. During Broomhall's lifetime evangelical Christians were to make a significant contribution to the removal of social injustices.

The importance of the Victorian age is best epitomized by the Great Exhibition, which Prince Consort Albert organised in Hyde Park in 1851. The visit of young Hudson Taylor and his sister Amelia to this exhibition on her sixteenth birthday is described later in this book.

Side by side with this exciting industrial and economic expansion came a remarkable growth in missionary endeavour. The spirit of enterprise and adventure which impelled people to explore and extend commerce also drove Christians to carry the Christian message to tribes and peoples who had not heard it. Technological advance became the handmaid of the missionary pioneers. Easier travel and more rapid communications assisted in the spread of Christianity. Railways and steamships carried the messengers of the Cross to new fields across the world. The cable and the telegraph improved communications between the distant mission stations and the home bases. The printing press could now be used effectively to inform the Christian public in Britain of the triumphs of the Gospel abroad, and also to publish newly translated portions of the Bible.

And so the age of scientific advance also became the age of the formation of great societies. Mainstream denominations as a whole were reluctant to take up the ever present challenge of entering new fields, and so voluntary societies, such as the Baptist Missionary Society, the London Missionary Society and the Church Missionary Society were formed to send out workers, though they had no formal links with the Baptist, Congregational and Anglican structures. One such voluntary society to be formed in this period was the China Inland Mission, which had no denominational backing. In 1875, ten years after its formation, Benjamin and Amelia joined its staff in north London.

At the time when Benjamin Broomhall came to work as a draper in London in the early 1850s, all kinds of developments were taking place in Christian missions, and his letters to his fiancee reveal that he was keeping abreast of such changes. David Livingstone, one of his heroes, had just carried out his exploratory travels in central Africa, and Benjamin went to hear him speak in the Exeter Hall. In India the BMS and CMS had been working for six decades, and had a church membership of 91,000. In the south Pacific strong churches had been formed by the LMS, the Paris Mission and the British Methodists. At missionary meetings of his Methodist Church in the Centenary Hall, 28 year old Benjamin Broomhall listened to encouraging reports from missionaries who had been working in South Africa and Fiji.

Protestant missionaries were just entering Japan and Korea, while in Burma the American Baptists had established a strong work among the Karen tribe. As Benjamin attended the annual May meetings of the large British societies he became enthused by the moving reports given by the missionary speakers. K.S. Latourette, the missionary historian, was later to describe the nineteenth century as 'The Great Century'. Christianity had been taken to more peoples than ever before, and had expanded to start including the whole globe and all ethnic groups.

When Benjamin Broomhall's future brother-in-law, Hudson Taylor, arrived in Shanghai in 1854 there were barely 200 Protestant Christians in China. The period of Benjamin's life was to be the period of important growth in church membership in the Chinese Empire, for when he died there were some 208,000 members in all societies.

In 1910, a year before Benjamin's death, the Edinburgh Missionary Conference was held, under the chairmanship of Dr. John R. Mott (who had been greatly influenced by Benjamin's book *The Evangelization of the World*). At this conference there was a spirit of optimism and excitement in the air in that, as a result of the missionary advances across the world in the nineteenth century, Christianity had now become a world religion. The ambitious theme of the Edinburgh Conference was 'The Evangelization of the World in this Generation', which was the watchword of the Student Volunteer Movement in the USA. The movement had been formed indirectly as a result of the distribution of Benjamin's book, and its watchword taken from its title.

It was Benjamin Broomhall's privilege to live in this exciting and important period in Christian missions, to work behind the scenes and see the activities of his own mission, the CIM, grow to become the largest Protestant mission in China.

2

The boy Benjamin

Staffordshire is seldom in the news. Those going on holiday pass through it, hardly noticing that they are in this peaceful county. Going by rail from London to north west England they will observe little but acre upon acre of farmland. If they go by car on the busy M6 through Staffordshire there is perhaps little to warrant stopping to sightsee.

Arnold Bennett, novelist of the Staffordshire Potteries, once wrote of his native county: 'England can show nothing more beautiful and nothing uglier than the works of nature and the works of man which are to be seen within the limits of this county.'

Our story begins in 1829 in the small village of Bradley (pronounced as 'Braidley'), some seven miles south-west of Stafford.

Life on a farm is never dull. Little Benjamin loved to talk with the farm-hands. One of them would help him on to his favourite horse, and gently escort him around the back yard. Soon the lad was riding confidently around the entire farm. Each horse in the Broomhall household had a nickname, and as a horse drank at the water trough on the side of the house Benjamin would talk to it. He sometimes milked the cows. He watched his father giving instructions to the farm-hands. As he got older he would accompany his father to the market-place in Bradley, and watch the buying and selling of farm products.

His father, Charles Broomhall, was a respected and prosperous farmer of a fertile area west of the river Penk. When Benjamin was later recalling the time when he was ten years old at the farm, he said, 'Those were days of prosperity with Father.' He went on to describe what would in those days be the trappings of wealth for a farmer. 'What a number of horses and cattle we had of all kinds. I remember at one time having six or seven riding horses. Father's business seemed to make Bradley a busy place.'

His father was not only a successful farmer, but also, in his spare time, an avid reader of books, and from him Benjamin also learned to enjoy sitting by the fire reading gripping stories. It is not clear what he read as we are told that Charles Broomhall did not allow his children to read fiction. He certainly read about the expansion of the British Empire across the world, and of the history and geography of foreign countries. He must have developed from his reading a vivid sense of imagination, and he in turn enjoyed entertaining his younger siblings, Ann, Charles and William before they went to bed with stories of his own inventing.

Later, in 1857, two years before he married, Benjamin looked back on his family life in Bradley, and paid tribute to the harmony and love he had known. He said, 'As a family, you might travel England through and through, and not find one more united in brotherly love and earnest desire to help each other. A jarring word I have not known for years.'

One of Benjamin's earliest recollections was of 'father's strictness and diligence in things spiritual'. This helped the lad to have a strong sense of security. He knew what actions or omissions would bring punishment, and what brought approval and encouragement.

When he spoke of 'diligence in things spiritual' he was referring to the Christian atmosphere of his childhood home. On Sunday mornings Charles Broomhall would take the children who were old enough to go, to the parish church, where he himself sang in the choir. After the service the vicar always had a friendly word for the Broomhall children, and would then pass on to Charles the latest book which he had been reading.

Sunday was a quiet day for this close family, which eventually numbered seven sons and one daughter, of whom Benjamin was the eldest. During the afternoon the local preacher who was to take the evening service at the small Primitive Methodist chapel would arrive at the farm, and have supper with them, after which, they went with him to the church on the edge of the farm. Charles always regarded himself as a kind of spiritual shareholder in the small chapel, for in 1839 he had given a site on his farm for the building, and had made a generous donation towards the purchase of the building materials.

Charles Broomhall was himself an accredited Primitive Methodist local preacher, and took his turn on the circuit plans to preach at the Bradley chapel and other chapels nearby. The important thing about his religious convictions was that he carried them into his workaday world. He had a strong sense of justice which in turn powerfully influenced young Benjamin, as we shall see in the unfolding of his life-work. Charles was known in the district for his honesty and kindness. The neighbouring farmers, while respecting him, resented the fact that his farm-hands received higher wages than theirs. They complained among themselves that they had been forced to raise their hourly rates in order to avoid their farm-hands seeking employment with Charles.

The fervour of the local society of Primitive Methodists had a strong influence on young Benjamin. Historically, this branch of Methodism had its roots in Staffordshire in 1811 — at Mow Cop, a hill to the north of the Potteries. Its founders were two humble artisans. But the county's links with Methodism went back to the movement's very beginnings.

John Wesley, the founder of Methodism, paid his first visit to Staffordshire in 1738, the epic year in which he had experienced his 'heart strangely warmed' at a London prayer meeting. His last visit to this county had been in 1790, a year before his death. His periodic visits to these parts had been fraught with personal danger. In 1743 he wrote in his journal about a visit to Wednesbury, in the south-east of the county. He recorded that the mobs had threatened to 'knock his brains out'.

Forty years after this particular visit he was encouraged to find that the Methodist people had grown in numbers. On 30 March 1784 (the year in which the Wesleyan Connexion was fully registered by law) he had written: 'I preached in the new meeting house at Harley Green. But this was far too small to hold the congregation. Indeed this county is all on fire, and the flame is spreading from village to village'.

Within six years of Wesley's death a series of secessions from mainstream Methodism began to take place. Some of these Methodist groups, as in other parts of Britain, were spreading through Staffordshire — Wesleyan Methodists (the original denomination), the Methodist New Connexion, and then the Primitive Methodists.

Our story relates to this last group, which commenced in this county and spread across it, known by its critics as 'the Ranters'. Their members tended to be people of limited means and little education. Their local preachers, who included both men and women, were people who could barely read. This is the point at which to introduce Bessie Haines, whom Benjamin later acknowledged as having had a great spiritual influence on the eight Broomhall children, even more than their mother (Jane). Bessie had been taken on as a dairy-worker at the family farm. She had proved to be an exceptionally good one, for it is recorded of her that 'her butter fetched a penny a pound more than any other'.

But although she could not read she was an accredited local preacher. Her heart was full of the joy of her faith, and as she worked in the dairy she sang Wesley's hymns with much gusto. To help Bessie prepare her sermons, Jane Broomhall used to read to her passages from Matthew Henry's popular *Commentary on the Bible*. Bessie loved the Broomhall children and became a vital part of the large family.

At first it was Benjamin's pleasant duty, as the eldest boy, to drive Bessie in his father's gig to her preaching appointments; and as the family grew up Charles and William were to have their turns. The journey to the service would involve a rehearsal of the sermon to be preached, and on the return journey the youthful driver would listen to a lecture on following Christ wholeheartedly. Bessie's talks were not resented because she had won everyone's hearts.

The first school to which Benjamin went was in Church Eaton, a few miles west of Bradley. Then he moved on to the local village school, where the schoolmaster, Cornelius Bridgett, spotted him as a promising student and as a boy with a strong religious background. His influence on young Benjamin must have been considerable, for when, some five years later, he learned that the teenager was moving to Barnsley to be apprenticed to a local draper, he went to the trouble of issuing his pupil with 'a testimony of respect'. What he wrote for the departing lad could have been a nineteenth century version of the book of Proverbs, and was treasured by Benjamin throughout his life:

> Never trust to your own understanding in the things of the world ...
> Value your Bible as your best treasure ...
> Maintain strict temperance and sobriety ...
> In every affair of life begin with God ...
> Make prayer a pleasure and not a task ...
> The approbation of Heaven and of your own conscience are
> infinitely more valuable than the applause of men ...

The valued advice ends with an appeal to 'read this over once a month' and 'to walk by these rules'.

These then were the powerful influences on this teenager as he left the sheltered home on the Bradley farm to enter his chosen trade of drapery — a secure and happy home, a godly father with a strong sense of justice, the simple sermons of Bessie, the warmth of a Primitive Methodist society and the fatherly advice of schoolmaster Cornelius Bridgett — all sound foundation stones for Benjamin's future active life. 'The flame of sacred love' could be traced to these early spiritual influences.

When he left home in 1844, not yet fifteen, his only sister Ann was thirteen, Charles ten, William seven, Edwin five, John one and a half. His mother was expecting her seventh child, Samuel. Four years later the family was complete with the birth of Henry.

3

Apprentice in Barnsley

Benjamin arrived in Barnsley just before his fifteenth birthday. It was a big step for a teenage boy to leave behind his home at Bradley and his warm family life. Barnsley was in the centre of the Yorkshire coalfields. The miners' cottages could be seen running in squat grey rows along the contours of the scrub-covered hills. He soon found the workmen tough but warm-hearted.

He had entered into an apprenticeship agreement with a local tailor, and was eager to do well in his chosen trade. He stayed with a Methodist couple, whose son William Till, was later to marry his sister Ann.

Benjamin had come from Bradley with the dual spiritual influence of the parish church and the Primitive Methodists. The former had taught him a love for orderliness in worship, and the latter the warmth of fellowship between those of like spiritual mind. On his first Sunday in his new environment he attended St. George's Church. Soon afterwards he joined the confirmation class. The vicar was careful to show that this step was not an empty formality, but a solemn declaration of faith.

It was inevitable that Benjamin should also visit the Wesleyan Methodist chapel. This whole area was 'Methodist country'. John Wesley had passed through Barnsley often in the late eighteenth century. Those had been dangerous days for the Methodist preachers. But a change of atmosphere had come through the godly lives of these preachers. On 30 June 1786, at the age of eighty-two, he had recorded in his journal: 'I turned aside to Barnsley, formerly famous for all manner of wickedness. They were then ready to tear any Methodist preacher in pieces. Now not a dog wagged his tongue. Surely God will have a people to Himself in this place.'

Half a century later Benjamin was to find Wesley's prophecy come true. When he came to this town God indeed had a people in Barnsley. It was here that he entered into full assurance of faith and never looked back. Two and a half years after his arrival, a service on the first Sunday of 1847 at the Pitt Street Wesleyan Chapel deeply touched the heart of this young man. The preacher spoke from the text 'How long will you halt between two opinions?' (I Kings 18:21). Benjamin was not normally an emotional or excitable person, but tears came down his cheeks. He told his fiancee, Amelia, 11 years later on the anniversary of this event, 'The moment of decision did not come until Mr. Roberts announced his text. ... The bare announcement of the text seemed enough. I don't remember a word of the sermon, but I know I went home most wretched.'

When he got home he went straight to his room. Although his future brother-in-law, William Till, did not know what had happened at church, he entered his room and asked, 'Benjamin, are you tired of serving Baal?' The following Sunday William took Benjamin with him to a class meeting in one of the vestries of the church. The young man recalls, 'My excellent friend, John Rollin, spoke to me, and I could not reply.' The meeting closed in good Wesleyan fashion with prayers being offered for him. 'I shall never forget that moment, the recollection affects me now.' 'The flame of sacred love' to his Saviour was to burn on for the rest of his life.

For Benjamin there was now no looking back. He found in the Methodist class meetings the instruction and fellowship which he needed, and remained a Wesleyan Methodist for the rest of his life. Marshall says, 'From the time of his conversion to the end of his days the ruling passion of his life was the salvation and moral welfare of mankind, and he began his helpful ministry among his own people.'

From time to time Benjamin paid visits back to his home in Staffordshire. His brothers were growing up, and farm life was much the same as when he was there. When it got around that Charles Broomhall's eldest son was home on a visit from Barnsley and would be preaching in the Primitive Methodist chapel, the villagers and farm-hands crowded into the little church. There was certainty and purpose in the young man's preaching, and he was eagerly heard.

Benjamin was disturbed to hear one day by letter that his father had stopped attending chapel and was no longer conducting family Bible reading. The nineteen year old son wrote a loving but pressing letter to his father: 'Your position in society requires that you should not only be decidedly pious yourself, but that you should set an example to your numerous observers by having family religion carefully and strictly attended to.' ...

During this period the draper's apprentice made friends with a lad who lived next door to his lodgings. Benjamin was nineteen and his new friend, Hudson Taylor, sixteen. His friend's father was James Taylor, the local pharmacist, and he seemed to the visitor to the home at 21 Cheapside to be a walking encyclopaedia — his general knowledge was phenomenal, and he could converse on almost any subject. A.J. Broomhall says that James Taylor was 'a great reader of theology, sermons, medicine and French literature'. He also had the capacity to memorize whole passages of a book. The young draper usually returned to his room with a book from James Taylor's library.

Among the many books the chemist had been reading was Basil Hall's *Voyage of Discovery along the Coast of China*. From this he had learned much about the Far East, and from this new knowledge he developed a concern for China to hear the Gospel. In their conversations with him, Hudson and Benjamin often heard him ask the question, 'The Methodists have sent missionaries to India and Africa. Why don't they send them to China?' As the friendship between the two teenage lads developed, Hudson often shared with Benjamin his innermost longings to be a missionary in China when he grew up. It was in the Taylor home that Benjamin first heard enthusiastic discussions about missions, and more particularly about those in China. For the rest of his life this was to become his most absorbing interest.

In his final years here Benjamin was an accredited local preacher, regularly taking services in the circuit. He visited the sick and gave counsel to those needing advice and help. In small ways he was being prepared for greater responsibilities in the years which lay ahead.

In his regular visits to the Taylor home, where he had virtually come to think of James Taylor and his wife as his parents, Benjamin had seen much of Hudson's sister, Amelia, six years younger than himself. She was attractive and intelligent, and she often joined in the discussions about foreign missions. Her love for Christ was apparent to all and her life was consistent with her profession. Whenever Benjamin confided his affections for Amelia in Hudson he received little encouragement, for his friend could not bear the thought of ever coming second in his sister's affections. The relationship between brother and sister was remarkably close. At fourteen Amelia left home to attend a small school in Barton on Humber run by her Aunt Hodson. Then her uncle, the Rev. Joseph Hudson, was widowed, and asked Mrs. Taylor if Amelia could stay in the vicarage at Dodworth to look after the children and his home. Over these years Benjamin only saw Amelia when she came home for brief holidays.

In 1851, two years after Amelia's departure to school, Hudson moved to Hull to work as dispenser to Dr. Richard Hardey, a distant relative. Amelia and Hudson had left Benjamin in Barnsley, where he visited the Taylor parents regularly. Hudson was in regular correspondence with the Chinese Evangelization Society, and was eager to get to China. A year after joining Richard Hardey he went to London, found some temporary work and continued his negotiations with the CES. Benjamin took a journey to London to see his friend who was feverishly preparing for his departure for China. They sang songs and hymns together, and reminisced on earlier days in Barnsley.

When Benjamin returned to Barnsley he was conscious of the strain which Hudson's parents were under regarding Hudson's imminent departure. Strangely enough, before their son was born the parents had prayed that he would serve God in China, but now that he was going their minds were in turmoil. Benjamin spent much of his spare time with Hudson's parents, assuring them that all would be well with their son. Was he not going at the call of God, and would he not therefore be protected and guided? Then the day came for James Taylor to travel to Liverpool to bid farewell to Hudson before his voyage. Father and son embraced, wept and prayed together. On 19 September 1853 Hudson Taylor sailed on the little three-masted clipper, S.S. *Dumfries*, for Shanghai, a six-month voyage.

Five months before Hudson Taylor set sail, Benjamin's sister Ann, had married William Till and settled in Barnsley. Benjamin boarded with them for a short period, in the following year, and then having qualified as a draper, he left Barnsley. Ann died in 1859. At the time of Benjamin's departure Amelia was still at the Dodworth vicarage. The young man moved briefly to Bradford, and then to London where he would be residing or working for the rest of his life.

4

Life in the metropolis

Benjamin Broomhall arrived in London in early 1854. He went into a drapery business at 20 New Bond Street. 'Bespoke' tailoring in London was carried on mainly in the West End area where his shop was situated. At that time six per cent of all London males and eight per cent of females were employed in work connected with clothing. Shop assistants and staff had to be in lodgings provided by their employers, and these were often insanitary and overcrowded.

His clients were the rich and influential in the high society of English life. They tended to be exacting in their demands for gentlemanly garb. In Victorian drapery good profits could be made in serving these wealthy and high-class citizens. Clyde Binfield has observed that in this period a number of drapers from humble Nonconformist backgrounds were upwardly mobile and prosperous by dint of hard work. They often became leading deacons and leaders in their churches. Such was to be the story of Benjamin Broomhall.

Tradesmen were flocking to the capital in search of good and secure jobs, but there was much in London which could lead such young men astray. There was a saying that the first 24 hours of a young man's life in London usually 'settled his eternity in heaven or hell'. After long working hours they would look for leisure and recreation in their new environment, but often ended up in public houses or sleazy night clubs. Drink and immorality were among the many temptations. The lodgings to which they returned at night were stinking tenements down darkened alleys.

Benjamin joined the Hinde Street Wesleyan Methodist church, and almost every night of the week was attending lectures given by famous men in the large auditoriums of the city. It was a good opportunity to hear the great preachers about whom he had heard so much. Charles Spurgeon was preaching to a full church in the New Park Street Baptist Chapel, Southwark, and a few years later would be building his spacious Metropolitan Tabernacle at Elephant and Castle. At Exeter Hall, the centre of evangelical England, there were lectures on a wide variety of subjects.

Soon after his arrival he discovered a fast-growing youth movement, the Young Men's Christian Association, which was doing an important work to counter the attraction of the many sordid centres where young people were being led astray. The YMCA had been formed by George Williams in 1844, ten years prior to Benjamin's arrival. With a sound understanding of the needs of youth and a progressive policy of character building, the association had organised sporting, social and religious activities. Branch after branch was being formed in the capital, and the movement was spreading to other cities in Britain, as well as to North America and Europe.

Benjamin attended Bible classes and educational lectures at the central YMCA, and took careful notes. As he became known to the leaders he soon had the opportunity of leading the Bible discussions and giving addresses on the work of missions. It was at this time he met the founder of the movement, George Williams, eight years his senior, with whom he formed a friendship which was to deepen over the following 50 years.

The two young men had much in common. While Benjamin had come from a Nonconformist chapel in Yorkshire, Williams had come to London from a similar chapel in Bridgwater, Somerset. They had both arrived in the capital as qualified drapers looking for wider opportunities in their trade. Williams had joined Hitchcock & Rogers, the fast-growing firm of retail drapers in Ludgate Hill. Both were preachers and keen students of the Bible, and both had a strong interest in foreign missions. Forty years later, Sir George Williams, would be chairing the annual meetings of the China Inland Mission, with Benjamin giving the Secretary's Report. But that is to jump ahead of our story.

Benjamin maintained his deep loyalties to his Wesleyan Methodist church, although it was going through a time of controversy. He was a trustee, and an accredited local preacher. He became his church's missionary secretary, and taught in the Sunday School. He attended the public meetings of the Wesleyan Methodist Missionary Society, and listened with keen interest to talks given by returning missionaries on their work abroad. In 1857 he attended one such meeting. Benjamin listened with amazement as James Calvert from Fiji recounted vividly how he had been wading across a reef at Viwa and was sur-rounded by 'armed savages' and been 'marvellously delivered'. Calvert was now in Britain supervising the printing of the Bible in Fijian. At the same meeting the Rev. William Arthur, later Secretary of the Wesleyan Methodist Missionary Society, closed in prayer with a sentence which moved him: 'Baptize some present for this work.' He commented in a letter to Amelia, 'I could scarcely repress my emotion.'

In 1854 Hudson Taylor wrote to Benjamin, 'I think you will join me sooner or later. Consider the use you could be out here. Oh, for the sake of Him who loved you even unto death, leave all, following Him, come out and engage in this important work.' The letters from his friend in China often ended with such pressing words, and Benjamin, sensitive young Christian as he was, had to consider this possibility seriously. Later Hudson wrote, advising ordination in order to have respect and recog-nition in China from other missionaries. He was speaking from painful experience. Hudson pointed out that his own church, the Wesleyan Methodists, still had no work in China. The English Presbyterians were too Calvinistic and the Anglicans too controlled by their bishops. But the missionaries of the London Missionary Society were of a high calibre and, like Benjamin, they were lovers of books and knowledge, and what was also important, they worked with a reasonable degree of freedom under their society.

Benjamin's response to these pressing pleas from Hudson was to consult a close friend, in whom he had great confidence, as to his suitability to be a missionary abroad. The carefully considered verdict which he received he regarded as final. He had other qualifications, his friend told him, than those required for a missionary, and these lay in personal and public relations. While the acceptance of his friend's assessment closed the door to his going to Africa, India or China, he was still convinced that for his life-work he would serve the cause of foreign missions at home in Britain, and exploit the gifts which his friend had identified.

Benjamin's shop in New Bond Street was prospering. Among his many profitable clients was the Charterhouse School, to which he supplied school uniforms. Was it not time to be considering marriage and setting up a home? He could never forget the gentle and attractive young lady, Amelia, the devoted sister of his close friend Hudson. It was a case of 'absence makes the heart grow fonder'. She was shy and retiring by nature, but had a keen mind and a firm commitment to evangelism and missionsary work. He had not seen her for several years, and wondered if she would respond to his love, or if she had changed since their last meeting. He told himself that if he could have her love and companionship he would indeed be fortunate. He had been praying about this for some time.

Following the Victorian etiquette of the day, he wrote to James and Amelia Taylor, with a degree of anxiety, asking if he could commence a correspondence with their daughter, Amelia. James Taylor's reply opened the door for which Benjamin was waiting: 'Having the highest opinion of your moral character and Christian deportment, I cannot but accede to your request. ...'

The consent was couched in formal language, but it was in the affirmative. As Marshall Broomhall says, 'The door into Paradise was opened.' Letters then flowed regularly between Barnsley and London with increasing freedom and warm expressions of love. A year later, in 1857, Benjamin and Amelia became engaged.

On the first Sunday of every year Benjamin attended the Covenant Service at his Methodist church, following an order prescribed by John Wesley in 1755. For this young man it was a renewal of the promises he had made at a New Year service in Barnsley ten years earlier. Solemnly and sincerely he would renew his covenant with Christ:

> I am no longer my own, but yours. Put me to what you will, rank me with whom you will. Put me to doing, put me to suffering. Let me be employed for you or laid aside for you, exalted for you or brought low for you. Let me be full, let me be empty. Let me have all things, let me have nothing. I freely and wholeheartedly yield all things to your pleasure and disposal.

Just after their engagement, Benjamin wrote to Amelia, 'I intend to send you a copy of the Covenant Engagement. Join me in spirit on Sunday in solemnly renewing this covenant with God. And oh, let us try to live through the week and through the year in its spirit.' This annual renewal of his covenant helped Benjamin to maintain his 'flame of sacred love' to his Lord and Master.

Both young people were anxious to be fully committed followers of Jesus Christ, and so in their letters they discussed such matters as whether Christians should go to the theatre, drink wine and sing 'merry and comic songs'. Jenny Lind, a famous Swedish soprano singer, had won popularity during her tour of Britain. Benjamin met her one day and she gave him a ticket to attend her farewell concert before departure. He wanted to hear her sing, he told Amelia in a letter, but could not accept the invitation because the programme included the singing of both sacred pieces and secular songs. The two could not be mixed. In his youthful zeal he was inclined to be dogmatic about such matters, but he mellowed as he got older.

But the theme most discussed in their love letters was the question of joining Hudson in China. Although Amelia knew of

Benjamin's firm decision, she was very vulnerable to Hudson's constant pleas to go out and help him, but would not dream of doing so if Benjamin could not change his mind. She wrote on one occasion: 'I want to mention the subject of China. ... Every time China is mentioned it brings the thought, ought we to go?'

Gradually she came to realise how definite her fiancé was about not becoming a missionary. He clearly felt the need to find a niche which would serve the work of missions at home in Britain. But the pleas from Hudson continued year after year, and it was difficult for Amelia to refuse her beloved brother.

Another topic constantly mentioned in the young people's love letters related to Hudson's well-being and safety. He had arrived in China when the Taiping rebels were rampaging through the central provinces, destroying and killing. Every item of news in the press about events in China was related to how it would affect their Hudson. Then came the disturbing news that he had had his head shaved and was wearing native dress. Amelia wrote to Benjamin that she was sickened to hear of this development. Benjamin sought to calm her anxieties. Most disturbing of all was the news in 1857 that, four years after his arrival in China, Hudson had resigned from the CES. He was now not only living in a dangerous political situation in a faraway land, but was a one-man band in this distant country, without any support. Little did Amelia and Benjamin realise how limited was the financial support which the CES had actually given him after his arrival in China.

Two years of regular correspondence came to a happy end. The young suitor took a journey to Barnsley, and on 10 February 1859 Benjamin Broomhall and Amelia Taylor were joined in holy matrimony.

5

Deliverance to the captives

Before we describe the early life of the lady who was to be Benjamin's life partner, let us consider in this chapter a worthy cause which fired the young man's imagination while still a bachelor in London, and which was to absorb much of his spare time for some 20 years.

Let us try to imagine a scene of panic and crisis in an African village in the mid-nineteenth century. The huts are in flames. Some villagers have been rounded up, while others, carrying small screaming children, rush out into the fields. Driven by terror, they hide in the long grass, or take shelter in caves, marshes, forests — wherever they can find a hiding place. Those who are of no value to the traders, because of age or ill health, are either murdered or left behind to starve. Those who have been rounded up — the healthy men, women and children — are put in chains in long lines, and ordered to march mile after mile in the boiling sun, goaded on with the lashes of whips. After hours of struggling along the rough roads, the slave prisoners arrive at the coast, where they are packed into the holds of Western ships amid heat, stench and constant discomfort. Many of them die of disease and overcrowding on the way to Western ports.

———————

The speaker graphically describing all this was David Livingstone, the famous missionary explorer, and his subject the evils of the slave trade. He had a large audience in the spacious Exeter Hall. Benjamin, recently arrived in London, was spellbound by what he heard and sickened by the lurid picture painted by the missionary. Livingstone gave a frightening statistic to his listeners: 'For each marketable slave that reaches the seaboard, ten lives are lost in the interior of the country.'

He turned towards the young men in the audience and said appealingly, 'All I can say to you to-day is: May Heaven's rich blessing come down on anyone — American, English or Turk — who will help to heal this open sore of the world.' He closed his moving address by asking, 'Can the love of Christ not carry the missionary where the slave trade carries the trader?'

Livingstone's ability to communicate his burden for the removal of such barbaric practices was such that the listeners crowded around him at the conclusion of the meeting to ask further questions. Benjamin Broomhall, overwhelmed by what he had heard, was able to have a brief conversation with the great explorer, an encounter which he never forgot.

He wrote to Amelia soon afterwards:

'What we can do is very little compared with the great work which is to be accomplished before slavery is abolished. But if we can help one poor soul into freedom and liberty, we shall not have laboured in vain. What a mountain of misery is crushing hundreds of fellow creatures with like feelings as ourselves. May God undertake for them, we can do but little.'

He went on to describe the brief discussion which he had had with Livingstone, and the effect which it had had on him. Amelia replied, 'It was very nice for you to speak to Dr. Livingstone. He must be a noble fellow, and in days to come, I dare say, you will have pleasure in thinking of even so short an acquaintance.'

───────────

The slave trade had become active in the eighteenth century. In 1774 John Wesley, founder of the movement to which Benjamin and Amelia belonged, had published his *Thoughts upon Slavery*, in which he asserted that 'no material considerations can justify the injustice and cruelty of the slave system'.

The British people had both defended and attacked the system, but evangelical Christians had fought the trade with much vehemence. In 1807, as a result of the campaigning of William Wilberforce and his fellow Evangelicals, slavery was finally abolished. Then in 1833, as a result of the work of T.F. Buxton and others, slaves throughout the British Empire were emancipated.

But Christians in Britain soon became aware that more slaves than ever were crossing the Atlantic. An active trade was still being carried on in East Africa, operated by Arab and Swahili people. Slavery was still strong in the southern states of the USA, as well as in areas controlled by France, Spain and Portugal. Between 1851 and 1856 Livingstone carried out his remarkable travels across Africa, and discovered to his dismay what the Arab slave trade was doing. Hence his desperate appeal at the Exeter Hall meeting.

The slavery issue was one of the first challenges that Benjamin faced when he came to the Metropolis. Just a year before his arrival Mrs. Harriet Beecher Stowe, author of *Uncle Tom's Cabin*, had also addressed crowded meetings at the Exeter Hall, as well as in other parts of the country. Her book was being widely read, and feelings were still high about the cruelties of the system when Benjamin arrived. From his earliest days on the Bradley farm and under the influence of his father, Charles Broomhall, he had developed a strong sense of justice and social righteousness. Whenever he witnessed any cruelty or exploitation he had always made a point of speaking directly to those concerned. For this he had not always been popular.

Benjamin had the temerity to seek out and interview Lord Shaftesbury. He was the Christian parliamentarian, who championed the cause of the exploited, whatever the sphere. This had included chimney sweeps, child beggars, 'cotton children', 'child slaves' in factories, as well as many such causes abroad, such as the conditions of factory workers in India. One of Lord Shaftesbury's biographers, John Kirton, describes him as 'a devoted abolitionist of slavery, a friend of the African race'. He was a man after Benjamin's heart, doing the kind of things which this young man would have done if he had been in Lord Shaftesbury's influential position.

The two men were one in their strictures of the conditions under which slaves had to work in the USA. But the wise statesman cautioned Benjamin about the danger of making criticisms of that country which were too harsh. 'After all,' Lord Shaftesbury observed, 'we share the sin of slavery with the United States. We compelled them, while they were under British rule, to receive the foul system into their provinces; and they only carried into effect what we, in our wickedness and folly, had forced upon them.'

Soon after this Benjamin joined the Anti-Slavery Association, and became its secretary. A number of anti-slavery organisations were formed in the mid-nineteenth century, differing from each other in strategy and purpose, and the one which Benjamin was to serve for nearly 20 years was small. It was his task to organise the meetings, write the minutes and conduct a large volume of correspondence. He wrote to Amelia, 'My hands are almost too full. I sometimes wish I was not secretary to the Anti-Slavery Association. It involves more work than anyone would suppose.'

But he saw that by undertaking this work he was making a humble contribution to the ending of the cruel trade. As he had earlier written to Amelia, he saw the slave trade as a 'mountain of misery crushing hundreds of our fellow creatures', and himself as doing a small but important part in bringing about its end.

The anti-slavery campaigners could soon see that the tide was turning in their favour. There was the American Civil War in the early 1860s in which the major issue was the ownership of slaves. On 1 January 1863 President Abraham Lincoln proclaimed the abolition of slavery, and this was followed by a series of abolition measures which ended the practice in the USA. At the Anti-Slavery Conference in Paris in 1867 the delegates had the satisfaction of being able to say: 'The slavery trade is diminishing everywhere. In the United States an immense event is being accomplished, and four million people have just entered the human family.'

Concern was expressed in this conference at the places where slavery was still being practised — Spain and Portugal and their colonies, Brazil, Turkey, Egypt, the Transvaal Republic and East Africa. Nevertheless the trade was rapidly waning.

Many anti-slavery campaigners then took up the cause of the opium trade being carried on between India and China. For Lord Shaftesbury it meant returning to a cause which he had championed as early as 1843, when as Lord Ashley he moved an important resolution in the House of Commons:[1]

> That it is the opinion of this House that the continuance of the trade in opium, and the monopoly of its growth in the territories of British India, is destructive of all relations of amity between England and China, injurious to the manufacturing interests of the country, by the very serious diminution of legitimate commerce, and utterly inconsistent with the honour and duties of a Christian kingdom, and that steps be taken as soon as possible, with due regard to the rights of government and individuals, to abolish the evil.

Benjamin also discontinued his anti-slavery work, feeling that the battle against such trade had now largely been won. Later in this story we shall see that he worked once again with Lord Shaftesbury, but this time in the fight against opium.

Notes

1. A.J. Broomhall, *Hudson Taylor and China's Open Century* (London, Hodder & Stoughton, 1989), volume 1, pp. 267, 268.

**An oil painting of Amelia Hudson Taylor as a girl by
Mrs. Richard Hardey of Hull.**

6

Enter Amelia

Amelia Taylor, three years younger than Hudson, was reared in a loving and intensely religious home. Frequently she saw her father, James Taylor, pacing the room behind the family shop dictating a sermon to his wife. Sometimes the local preachers gathered for meetings in the home at 21 Cheapside. Amelia enjoyed listening to their discussions on preaching, theology and politics.

Curly-headed Hudson taught her to take her first faltering steps in walking. The brother and sister sometimes played 'church', with Hudson standing on a chair holding forth while Amelia formed the attentive congregation. Very early in life the two developed an exceptionally close and loving relationship, which deepened as they grew older. In those early years they would go together to nearby Lunn Woods, where they chased butterflies and picked flowers. Hudson collected insects which he preserved in his father's pill boxes. He was intensely interested in nature and wild life, and Amelia shared in his many hobbies. When she went to bed Hudson would sit beside her and tell her simple stories until she was ready to drop off to sleep.

As was common in those days before compulsory school education, Hudson, Amelia, and later Louisa, had most of their schooling at home; their father teaching arithmetic, French and Latin, while their mother taught them English, music and natural history. There were other equally valuable lessons which they learned outside of lesson time. Slogans often rang in their ears which helped them to form good habits early in life — such as 'Learn to dress quickly', 'Always be prompt' and 'See if you can do without it.'

As Hudson and Amelia grew older they began doing simple acts of Christian service, such as giving out tracts in a poor part of Barnsley. They enjoyed attending Methodist gatherings and witnessed the celebrations of the centenary of the formation of Methodism. But when Hudson went to work in the local bank — his first exposure to the outside world — he was influenced by the scoffing and jeering of his fellow-clerks against Christianity, and he in turn became sceptical and materialistic, as well as irritated by having to attend family prayers.

All this hurt Amelia, who began to pray fervently for her brother's conversion. Her prayers were answered. One day when Hudson was free from his work he found a tract in his father's library which arrested his attention. It spoke of 'the finished work of Christ on the Cross' and led to his conversion. This was in May 1849, when Hudson was seventeen years of age. Within a few days he shared the news with Amelia, who rejoiced to hear it. She was to be his confidante and close adviser for the rest of his life. The brother and sister now grew even closer to each other.

But four months later, as already recounted, Amelia went to a small boarding school in Barton upon Humber, which was run by her mother's sister, Mrs. Hodson. Hudson and Amelia kept in touch by letter, and saw each other from time to time.

After his year at the bank, Hudson assisted his father in the chemist shop; and then at the age of nineteen he went to Hull to work for Dr. Robert Hardey, a distant relative. As a present for her sixteenth birthday Hudson took his sister to London for a week to see the Great Exhibition. Queen Victoria's husband, Prince Albert, had had the novel idea of organising a large scale exhibition to display to the world Britain's greatness and leadership in industry and technology. He chose a site in Hyde Park, and on it Crystal Palace was built in which were erected exhibits of modern inventions. On 1 May 1851 Queen Victoria

James Hudson Taylor (1832–1905).

had performed the opening ceremony, and excursion tickets brought thousands from other parts of Britain to the Metropolis. The average daily attendance was estimated at no less than 43,000.

The two young people from Yorkshire had to push their way through the milling crowds to see the many exhibits, which were of particular interest to Hudson's enquiring and scientific mind. They walked mile after mile through London seeing the historic sites of the capital — Westminister Abbey, the Tower of London and Regent's Park. But Hudson had an additional purpose in coming to London. He wanted to meet the leaders of the Chinese Evangelization Society, with whom he had been corresponding, and to speak to them about his desire to join the society and work in China. It had almost become an obsession. Amelia, while sharing her brother's interest in missions in China, was apprehensive about his going. The Taiping rebels were continuing to cause devastation and death everywhere they went. Was it wise to be making such plans? She was very protective of her brother.

On the Sunday following their visit to the Great Exhibition, they went by horse-bus to the village of Hackney to meet George Pearse of the CES. They went to the Breaking of Bread service at the Brethren assembly in Tottenham, and were made to feel very much at home. There they met a German missionary from China, Mr. Wilhelm Lobscheid, who gave Hudson little encouragement about becoming a missionary. Perhaps Amelia was quite relieved.

As has already been recounted, three years after the visit of brother and sister to London, Hudson Taylor sailed for China. The correspondence between the two continued to be regular and intimate. In a sense Hudson exercised a high degree of control over his sister's movements and decisions. He desperately wanted her in China, but as her relationship with Benjamin developed Hudson realised that his influence over her was waning.

So close was brother to sister that when Benjamin proposed to Amelia he felt duty-bound to write to Hudson in China for his approval. On 27 April 1856 Hudson wrote from Swatow to Amelia:

> In answer to his wish that I too would approve of his step, I told him I should regret anything which would prevent your labouring for the benefit of the females of China. But apart from that I knew no one to whom I would sooner see you united, and that I was not without hope of seeing him in China.

In other words, Hudson Taylor approved of the engagement of Amelia and Benjamin if it brought them as workers to China. But neither of them ever went to that land.

Hudson also did not think that Benjamin had a secure enough future in the drapery trade to be thinking of marriage. He went on to say:

> If Benjamin does not mean to come out, what are his views and plans for the future? Without money it is not easy, I should think, to commence in his business. I do not much relish the idea of your staying behind a draper's counter. As to your leaving poor mother, I don't know what to think of it. You are her only comfort.

But when Hudson proposed to Maria Dyer soon after this, he had even less to offer.

This then is the background to the young lady who became Benjamin Broomhall's wife and the mother of his ten children. Her intense loyalty to Hudson had to give way to her becoming a wife to Benjamin Broomhall. From now on her story is absorbed in their common life of devotion to the work of God.

The newly-weds purchased a house at 63 Westbourne Grove, Bayswater, which was fast becoming a rural suburb of London. This was to be their home for 12 years, from 1859 to 1871. It was here that seven of their children were born — Gertrude, Hudson, Emily, May Louise, Marshall, Edith and Alice. Bayswater was one of the villages to which the Metropolis was pushing its way out, and gradually houses were going up on Notting Hill where there had once been virgin parkland. Benjamin walked to his drapery business down the Bayswater Road to Oxford Street and New Bond Street.

My cousin, Mrs. Alice Forrest, records of this period of Benjamin's and Amelia's lives,

> The Broomhall family were expected, not only to go to the Wesleyan chapel on Sundays, but to assist in mission hall services in the East End. Because they were strict Sabbatarians, they would walk many miles along the hard London pavements, carrying not only their heavy Bibles, hymn books and tracts, but medical supplies for the sick and the drunks whom they encountered, giving a practical aspect to their ministry. This experience the children were to find most useful in their later missionary work in China.

Even before his marriage Benjamin had been helping the Methodists to establish a work in the Bayswater area. He wrote to Amelia on 15 December 1858:[1]

> On Saturday evening I took tea at Mr. William Arthur's house, on the occasion of the first meeting of the trustees etc. belonging to the new chapel. Mr. Punshon, Mr. Macdonald, Mr. Budgett and others, making about twenty, were there. Mr. Macdonald asked me if I was aware that it was the dying request of Mr. Goodfellow that I would take his Sunday Afternoon Class. Mr. Arthur said he hoped I should have no hesitation in complying... I have decided to take the class. Mr. Punshon told me that he had fixed for Secretary of the Branch Missionary Society, which he hoped to see organised soon. I have also been appointed member of the Sunday School Committee ... So you see I am becoming more identified with Methodism — already a trustee, leader, missionary secretary etc.

Mentioned in the letter were two Methodist ministers with whom Benjamin was to work closely — Rev. W. Morley Punshun, LL.D. and Rev. William Arthur. Morley Punshon served the Bayswater Church from 1858 to 1861. Benjamin Broomhall, the keen young Methodist local preacher, learned much about preaching from this pastor, who had both a brilliant command of English and a memory which enabled him to quote from various sources with little recourse to his notes. He was famous for his four sermons on 'The Prodigal Son' which were later published.

Frail and fervent William Arthur influenced Benjamin in a different way. He had briefly been a missionary in India, but had been forced through ill health to return to Britain. But Mr. Arthur never ceased to be a strong advocate of the missionary cause. He shared with Benjamin, not only the urgency of spreading the Gospel, but also the cause of Temperance, and a strong support for the northern states in America in the fight against slavery. Benjamin's spiritual life was challenged by William Arthur's best-known book *The Tongue of Fire*, a copy of which he sent to Hudson Taylor in China.

The church was built in Denbigh Road, just around the corner from the Broomhalls' home. It was convenient for Sunday worship, and also for the many activities in which Benjamin was now involved. Soon a Bayswater Circuit was formed with societies also in Warwick Gardens, Clarence Place, Kensal Town and Starch Green. The minutes of the Bayswater Circuit record that before long there were 360 members in the Bayswater society, 285 Sunday School scholars and 35 teachers. The records also show that Benjamin regularly attended the meetings of the Bayswater Circuit, which took place at the Denbigh Road Chapel, until September, 1867.

At this time Benjamin and Amelia became members of the Westbourne Grove Baptist Chapel, whose pastor, the Rev. W.G. Lewis was the Editor of the Baptist Missionary Society Magazine, and served on the society's committee. The pastor's active interest in missions in China attracted the young couple to worship at the church.

A year after they settled into their new home in Bayswater they had a pleasant surprise, and their neighbours had a surprise of a different kind. Early one morning in 1860, down the road came a tall Chinese man, carrying an English baby. He was accompanied by an English woman carrying some bags. Behind them was a short man in Chinese clothes, also carrying luggage.

In the months which followed the neighbours were to see these strange people coming and going from No. 63.

The four people were in fact Wang Lae-djun, Taylor's assistant in translation work, sixteen-month-old Grace, and Maria and Hudson Taylor. The tired travellers were given a warm welcome in the Broomhall home. Amelia was meeting Maria, Hudson's wife, for the first time. Both she and Hudson had to get used to the other one now having a spouse, and loving and deep relationships were soon formed. Hudson found in the Rev. W.G. Lewis a useful contact with the BMS, and Hudson and Maria became members of the church. It was Lewis who persuaded Hudson to use the title 'Reverend'.

Hudson Taylor at this time was in the invidious position of belonging to no society. He had a definite programme of work to do while he was in England — the translation of part of the Scriptures into the Ningbo dialect, the printing of a Ningbo hymn book, writing articles about China in missionary magazines, the completion of his medical studies in order to have a recognised qualification, the finding of recruits to go to China and above all, to pray and plan about his future in China.

Early in 1865 Hudson wrote a book, *China: Its Spiritual Need and Claims*, which was to become a best seller and to have a wide influence on Christians in Britain. In it he presented some statistics about the needs of China in a dramatic way: 'If all the Chinese were to march past a spectator at the rate of 30 miles a day, they would move on and on, day after day, week after week, month after month. Over seventeen years and a quarter would elapse before the last individual passed by.' Such a picture showing the enormous population of the Chinese Empire could not fail to impress the Christian public.

It was in June of that year that Hudson Taylor, needing a rest, went to Brighton. Walking along the beach one Sunday morning, he asked God for 24 fellow workers, and a few days later opened an account at the London and County Bank, and deposited £10 in the name of 'China Inland Mission'. It was a small initial step of faith, hardly noticed at the time by Christians in Britain, but it was a case of 'despise not the day of small things'.

A year later things had developed considerably. Taylor booked the S.S. *Lammermuir*, an up-to-date square-rigged sailing ship with an iron frame and three masts, to take him, his family and his first recruits to Shanghai. On 26 May 1866, the travellers assembled at the East India Dock, and embarked. A group of well-wishers saw them off, and among them were Benjamin and Amelia Broomhall and their three year old son, Hudson. Little Hudson never forgot the sight of the departing missionaries, and 18 years later he himself sailed with his sister Gertrude to serve in his uncle's mission.

Just after the birth of their seventh child, Alice, Amelia had a vision of Christ which stayed with her for the rest of her life. In a short autobiography she recalled:

> I had a wonderful vision of Christ ... I could dimly discern a figure slowly emerging into greater clearness, and oh! the rapture of that moment, it was my Saviour. I have never lost the memory of that Face, nor the influence of beholding it. Even at this distance of time it brings tears to my eyes and warms my heart. I have sometimes asked that it might be repeated. The thought of that Face brings heaven nearer, makes it more real, and robs death of its sting.

Her son, Marshall, says, 'From this time onward she lived as seeing Him who is invisible, and she conversed in prayer as with an unseen but ever present friend.' Amelia's 'flame of sacred love' had been fanned by this precious vision of her Saviour.

It was in 1871 that the Broomhall family moved to Godalming in Surrey. Benjamin continued to commute to his business in the West End. Marshall recalled that he had happy memories of this country home — 'the lovely garden with its fir tree ... the long walks in the country with the governess, Miss Wilkin ... the country chapel, and the carrying of a hot dinner to some sick person on Sundays'. Benjamin was again active in the local Methodist church.

The drapery business had been going reasonably well for many years, but the time came when the shop was no longer able to pay its way. The partnership broke up, and the receiver had to be called in. This was not easy for a man with a large family to support and a country home to maintain. From now on he continued his business from his home in Godalming, and it was here that an unexpected development took place which opened the door to Benjamin and Amelia working for God in an important sphere of service in which they were to find much fulfilment.

Notes

1. M. Broomhall, *Heirs Together of the Grace of Life* (London, Morgan & Son and CIM, 1915), pp. 56, 57.

7

I have found my destiny

It was in the year 1875 that Benjamin found the work for which his abilities and skills were admirably suited, the niche in which all his earlier training and environment found fulfilment.

For many the call of God to Christian service comes in childhood, and every step in the youthful years is taken with this in view. St. Paul speaks in Philippians 3 of the yearning of Christians to fulfil that purpose for which Christ had saved them. 'I keep going on, trying to grasp that purpose for which Christ Jesus grasped me' (J.B. Phillips).

But some find this divine calling in the more mature years of life. Ten years prior to Benjamin's turning point, a 36 year old Methodist minister, father of six, was returning home late at night along the streets of East London. There was a sparkle in his eyes and a spring in his step. He burst into his home and greeted his wife Catherine with the exciting announcement, 'Darling, I've found my destiny'. In William Booth's heart had been born the Salvation Army, with its subsequent worldwide programme of feeding the hungry and saving souls.

The call for Benjamin Broomhall also came later in life, at the age of forty-six.

In 1875 on a bright spring day Benjamin and Amelia were doing their work in their comfortable home in leafy Godalming. They had been in this attractive Surrey countryside for four happy years. Here Noel, Annie Marie and two-month old Benjamin had been born, bringing the family to ten, a not uncommon size for those days. Benjamin was at his desk, Amelia busy in the kitchen. The much loved governess, Miss Wilkin, was teaching the older children. It was a beautiful May day, and the children were looking forward to their usual afternoon walk down the country road, picking flowers and playing hide-and-seek behind the trees.

There was a knock at the door — a familiar knock and a welcome one. Amelia's hopes were confirmed. It was her brother Hudson. He was looking drawn and strained. She knew that he had had weeks in bed, and even in his illness he had had to make far-reaching decisions and interview candidates for the mission from his bedside. The pressures of a far-flung work were clearly taking their toll. The China Inland Mission had been going now for nine years.

As Benjamin, Amelia and Hudson drank tea and ate some freshly baked buns it was evident that the visitor had business to discuss. In a sense he was 'hitting them when they were down', for in his pocket was a letter received from Benjamin a fortnight earlier sharing the problems of his business life, and the tight budget involved in feeding and clothing ten growing children without the profits from the New Bond Street shop. Benjamin looked out of the window across the fields as his brother-in-law made an all too familiar pressing appeal to the couple:

> The work is growing in China. Few workers are coming forward to help meet these needs, and some already in the mission are proving to be problems to the work. Benjamin told me in a recent letter that his clothing business was not running smoothly. Why don't you both come out to China and help in the work there. I know that you would prove so useful at this critical time.

Amelia looked wistfully at her husband. She was vulnerable and sensitive to such appeals, and would have gone many years earlier to China, before she and Benjamin had even married, but her husband had always firmly refused. Hudson had been pressing them both at regular intervals for the past 20 years, perhaps with undue pressure.

But Benjamin would not go back on the decision he had made back in 1856, nearly 20 years earlier. He had gone to a trusted friend, someone whose advice he always valued, and asked him for his frank opinion as to whether he was suited for the mission field. His friend had strongly advised against such a step. 'You have qualifications of a different kind. You must do work involving public relations.' That had been enough for him, though he could not see when an opportunity could arise for doing the kind of work his friend assured him he was suited for.

And so once again it was a firm refusal, and Hudson could see that he really meant it. The fact that a business partnership had failed did not mean that Benjamin should go back on a decision he had prayerfully made in earlier years.

But Hudson, having failed in his opening gambit, clearly had another proposition to make. Amelia poured out some more tea as her brother proceeded to make a further appeal to them. The expression on Benjamin's face indicated that he did not think that Hudson's further suggestion, whatever it might be, would be any more helpful than the first.

Since the retirement of William Berger three years earlier, the voluntary helpers at the London office had not run the affairs of the mission well. The allocation of duties had not been suitably arranged, and Benjamin's skills were urgently needed or the growing work would suffer. It was essential to supply the churches and mission supporters with regular information about the work in China, and with his peripatetic life Hudson had only been able to issue at irregular intervals an '*Occasional Paper*'. With the CIM now reaching its tenth anniversary he was about to issue a regular magazine, *China's Millions*. Whilst he as founder would want to write the important articles, someone was needed to insert extracts from the letters and reports received from missionaries on the field, co-ordinate the material, check the draft copies and supervise the magazine's distribution. Again Benjamin was surely the man for the job.

Turning to Amelia, Hudson described the need for a mother to ensure the smooth-running of the catering at the mission home. There were missionaries passing through needing assistance, there were young lady candidates feeling homesick as they prepared for their long journey to the East. There would be a constant flow of visitors coming to the home. Was this not a service which Amelia could do for her Master?

Turning his attention back to Benjamin, Hudson continued his job description. There were churches wanting deputation meetings, and someone was needed to arrange for missionaries on furlough to take these meetings. Someone skilled in dealing with ministers and church leaders was urgently needed. There were families in which problems had arisen in connection with the departure of young men and women to China. There were conventions where the mission would have to be represented to stake the claims of its work. As Benjamin listened to this he asked himself if this was not the type of work in public relations which his friend had advised him he was well suited to do. Administration, journalism, dealing with the Christian public, selecting candidates — were these not just the kinds of work for which he had a genuine aptitude?

By now the attention and interest of Amelia and Benjamin had been won. They looked at each other, and then at Hudson. This would mean leaving their beloved home in Godalming. Could they support ten children on a missionary allowance? Hudson Taylor realised that such practical matters would be uppermost in their minds, but he was also aware of the danger of appearing to show favouritism to his close relatives. So he made a guarantee of a house in Pyrland Road and a regular income, an arrangement which would place them outside the normal conditions of service for the mission.

The couple could not conceal their interest in the proposition just put to them. They went carefully with Hudson through all the aspects of such a radical change of lifestyle. Their questions were answered carefully and frankly. Amid calls from the children for attention, they knelt together, and the mission leader led them fervently in prayer for guidance in every aspect of this far-reaching decision.

Forty-six year old Benjamin and his forty-two year old wife had found their destiny. In a real sense, in view of recent business reversals, they needed the appointment as a solution to their family commitments. But in a greater sense the work needed them — their capacity for shouldering the responsibilities which Hudson had outlined to them, their spiritual commitment which such a job required of them, and their personal dedication at this crucial stage in the mission's history.

8

The year 1875 a turning point ...

When Benjamin and Amelia arrived at Pyrland Road in north London, headquarters of the China Inland Mission, the move involved far-reaching changes.

First of all, came changes for this large and happy family. They had left behind the spacious and comfortable home in Godalming, Surrey, where they had spent four happy years, and where Noel, Annie Marie and Benjamin, Jun. had been born. They had left behind family privacy to become part of a large missionary family. They had left behind Miss Wilkin, the beloved governess of the children, and walks with her into the woods.

Amelia, in addition to being mother of the ten children, now had to be house-mother to a steady stream of candidates preparing to go to China. She would have to comfort young ladies who were leaving home to go to a strange and unknown distant land. She had to help Benjamin as he rushed off to take meetings all over the country. Her husband was inclined to leave home at the last minute in time just to catch a train about to leave. She always advocated leaving plenty of time and allowing for delays. The home often rang with the anxious words, 'Benjamin, if you don't leave now you will miss your train!'

Amelia was also to supervise the household staff and entertain the many visitors who came for information about the mission. She would welcome the newly-arriving candidates from far and near and make them comfortable. Soon an effective teamwork emerged. Amelia supervised the young people upon their arrival, and then, when they had been accepted by the London Council, Henrietta Soltau took them over for training at her nearby institute.

Amelia resolved from the start that, amid the volume of work which now fell on her shoulders, she would not neglect her ten children. She gave the older ones regular lessons, whilst Noel, Annie Marie and Benjamin, Jun. all under three, needed special love and attention.

As the number of candidates increased, so the dining-room became more crowded. Gertrude, Hudson and Emily would sometimes have to eat standing up in the kitchen. Marshall later recalled, 'Some of the privacies of home were lost, and not always willingly by us youngsters, but what a harvest of blessing was gained thereby.' The recently-arrived candidates loved the Broomhall children, and many were the romps that they had with them.

Within three years of their arrival Amelia's 'family' increased even further. She had always felt guilty that she had never gone out to China in response to Hudson's pleas for her help on the field. But an opportunity arose for her to make right in some measure her earlier failure, as she saw it. Jennie Taylor was anxious to return and rejoin busy and hard-pressed Hudson in China. So Amelia made an offer, so characteristic of her unselfishness. 'If Jennie is called to go to China, then I am called to care for her children.'

In one swoop her family had risen from 10 to 17. This merger of two families proved to be a happy mix of two sets of cousins. Gertrude Broomhall and Herbert Taylor were of the same age; Hudson Broomhall and Howard Taylor likewise; Marshall and Edith Broomhall and Maria Taylor were close in age; likewise Alice Broomhall and Charles Taylor. Benjamin Broomhall and Ernest Taylor were close in age, with Amy Taylor a year younger. Two year old Amy was sick with whooping cough, and needed special attention. Marshall later observed, 'When our cousins came to live with us we were a happy, rollicking family.'

In spite of having an enormous family to care for, Amelia made a point of finding time to pray with each child individually. In a booklet she wrote later she explained what she did: 'I made it a rule to take my children, one at a time, into my room; and then, before my child, would pour out my soul to the Lord.' She would confess any mistakes she had made in her dealings with that child, and tell the Lord what lessons she thought that child needed to learn. In a sense parts of Amelia's prayers were disguised lectures!

Amelia also held simplified church services with the children in her bedroom, based on the Methodist liturgy with which she was so familiar. In between the singing of the recently published Sankey hymns they would have a solemn service of Holy Communion. Each child took the bread and said, 'I take this in remembrance that Christ died for me, and am thankful.' And so with the wine. The service would end with a prayer, 'God bless Daddy as he preaches in Birmingham. Bless Uncle Hudson and Aunt Jennie far away in China, and protect them. ...'

But the move to London not only brought a change in the lifestyle and routine of the Broomhall family, but subsequent history has shown that the year 1875 ushered in a new era for the CIM.

Upon his appointment to the London Council, Benjamin Broomhall sprang to life with a new sense of purpose. It was only nine years after the formation of the mission and the departure of the ragtag *Lammermuir* group, and the mission was at a low ebb. The workers in China were dispirited with problems of culture shock, strained relationships, loneliness and disease. The work of the mission in Pyrland Road was slow and inefficient. Voluntary workers had done their best to keep the administrative side of the mission going, but there were glaring gaps of tasks left undone, as well as overlap and confusion in other spheres.

The public image of the CIM was poor. In some quarters it was dubbed 'the pigtail mission', referring to the founder's rule that every male missionary had to wear Chinese dress and have pigtails. Others used the mission's initials teasingly as 'constantly in motion', relating to the brave walks of missionaries across the breadth of China. One speaker in the House of Lords referred to Hudson Taylor as an 'incurable idiot' and his workers as 'a troop of novices'. One mission supporter admitted in later years, 'We were just emerging from a position of contempt and derision when Benjamin Broomhall joined the work, and his labours and wise advocacy did a great deal towards clearing away misunderstandings of ignorance.'

Benjamin by nature was sociable and good in all aspects of public relations work. Dapper in appearance and well spoken, he mingled with high society in London, many of the contacts having come from his drapery business in New Bond Street and his earlier work in the Anti-Slavery Association. He proved to be an able apologist for the mission with titled gentlemen and their families. Many a breakfast was held in such homes, and many letters from his pen went to people who were important in the public life of Britain.

Hudson had made numerous contacts in the early years with fine and dedicated Christians in the Christian Brethren, such as in the large assembly at Tottenham. Benjamin, with his deep roots in Anglicanism and Methodism and his reading of the journals of the mainstream denominations, brought the mission into the circle of these churches, with which he arranged deputation meetings and from which came the candidates in the years which followed. Typical of his ecumenical spirit was a statement which he made at a crowded meeting in Exeter Hall (later described), 'We in the CIM have the strongest sympathy with every evangelical mission in China. In the words of Wesley, "We are friends of all, and enemies of none".'

He counted among his friends bishops, moderators and presidents of these churches, as well as many local church pastors. These friends included the Rev. Handley Moule, Principal of Ridley Hall, Cambridge, and later Bishop of Durham; Eugene Stock of the Church Missionary Society; Dr. F.B. Meyer, Baptist minister of Regent's Park Chapel, Regent's Park; George

Williams of the newly formed YMCA. For his spiritual food he loved to read the sermons of Charles Spurgeon, R.W. Dale, A. McLaren and J.H. Jowett.

With his eirenic spirit and extrovert nature, Benjamin was able to present to the Christian public the picture of a mission which had a clear programme to evangelize China, and with a structure ready for growth as well as for crisis situations. His 20-year tenure as General Secretary was to be the golden age of the mission which he served with undiminished vigour.

Clearly, in God's providence, Benjamin and Amelia had arrived at just the right time. Their grandson, the historian of the mission, Dr. A.J. Broomhall, says that 1875 was 'the point at which the tide of all missions to China turned. ... The dawn of 1875 brought in the age of Protestant missionary expansion.' The effects of the 1859 Revival were such that by 1875 all missionary societies were beginning to receive more candidates.

In his earlier business life Benjamin had, in spite of his many skills, an inability to handle what would today be called budgets and cash flow, and had failed as a result. Also, he was known to lack promptness in keeping appointments and deadlines. These risks Hudson had knowingly taken when appointing him to the London staff, but he soon saw that, in spite of these known weaknesses, the step of faith he had taken in approaching Benjamin had been amply justified.

It was undoubtedly a case of the right person being in the right place at the right time.

Notes

1. Maria Taylor died in 1870, and Hudson Taylor married Jane Faulding in 1871.

9

The man in action

The missions of Dwight L. Moody were responsible under God for the general quickening of religious life in England in the 1870s. Henry Drummond, Scottish evangelist and fellow labourer, spoke of the permanent after-effects of Moody's meetings as influencing 'every field of social, philanthropic and religious activity'.

In 1873 Moody sailed for the British Isles for a two-year tour which made him a national figure. He invaded London for a four-month period during which the attendances totalled more than two and a half million. Moody, a folksy, rotund man with a fund of effective anecdotes, captured the imagination and won the affection of the reserved British public. With the help of Sankey he taught the people to sing experiential and lively hymns. Religion had become something happy and exciting.

These missions brought about a noticeable change in the attitude of Christians to their responsibilities in spreading the Gospel. New missionaries of many denominations began going out to new fields. The Church Missionary Society, for one, had a stream of new workers going to Africa and India.

In China there was a total of 436 missionaries of all societies, but the turnover was high with resignations, breakdowns in health and death by disease. The CIM had a total of only 38 missionaries, of whom 12 were on leave in Britain, recovering from a term of danger and overwork. The founder was directing the affairs of the mission from a sick-bed in Pyrland Road —

writing reports, articles and letters, interviewing candidates and giving Chinese classes to prospective missionaries.

The minutes of the London Council in 1876 stated that Benjamin was to spend much of his time in holding meetings in the country on behalf of the mission, together with such missionaries as might be home on furlough.

In his new appointment Benjamin sprang into action. Using the many contacts in the churches which he had made in his earlier 20 years in London, he began making whistle-stop tours of the country. He would take a missionary on furlough with him to a church with which he had already made arrangements for a meeting. After introducing the missionary, he would go to a nearby town and make further appointments before returning to join in the meetings at the first centre. When the missionary had been escorted to the second town, Benjamin would proceed to make contacts in yet another town. With this strategy a group of towns would be covered in one round trip, and news of the work of the CIM shared with an ever-widening circle of Christians of various denominations.

Working at his desk in Pyrland Road, Benjamin would carefully acknowledge each donation, large or small, in his flowing handwriting, before passing the funds on to William Soltau, the cashier and accountant. Marshall tells us that his father kept a large Letts' Diary in which he recorded extracts from donors' letters. Gifts ranged from four pence to a shilling. Extracts were written from letters received from widows, children and working men. At a private breakfast gathering in the West End home of T.A. Denny, at which eight persons were present, Benjamin took from his pocket a letter which had touched him deeply. It was from a poor widow in Scotland. 'I can do without meat', she wrote, 'but the heathen cannot do without the Gospel.' Whereupon his host said that all he had ever given to the work of God had never cost him a mutton chop. He gave Benjamin £500 for the work of the mission in China. Others present made similar gifts, and the total came to £2,500.

Soon after Benjamin and Amelia joined the mission it experienced wave after wave of new missionary recruitments. It was essential that the mission had a sound administrative base to handle such a volume of recruits, and the couple established a strategy for handling such a rush of candidates. Without this the events of the subsequent years would have ended in chaos.

In 1875 there was a call from Hudson Taylor, after much prayer and consultation, for 'Eighteen New Workers'. Aware with hindsight of the problems experienced with some of the *Lammermuir* group, the founder stipulated that applicants should have a basic education and be able to mix socially with all classes. In the first decade of the CIM's history only three provinces had been occupied — Zhejiang, Jiangsu and Anhui. The 'Eighteen' would be needed in nine pairs to enter the other nine provinces. Some workers on the field, finding the mission's allowance quite inadequate, considered 'The Call' irresponsible. The more mouths there were to feed, the less was available to go round.

For Benjamin and Amelia this call involved a wide range of extra responsibilities — corresponding with the applicants, visiting their home churches, arranging interviews, providing accommodation. When the 'Eighteen' had been chosen they found that more than 60 applicants had been interviewed. Those who had been accepted went bravely at Christ's call to the great unknown. They were to prove good workers, exploring new provinces and carrying out effective evangelism.

But that was only the first wave. More were to come. Hudson Taylor was a visionary who could conceive of nothing less than every province of China being evangelized and having strong indigenous local churches, and this required more and more workers. In 1881 Hudson was in Wuhan. He was walking on a hill outside the town with A.G. Parrott, discussing the size of the task and the missionaries available. There were now 96 members in the mission. Hudson quoted to Parrott from Luke 10:1: 'After these things the Lord appointed other seventy also ...' Were 70 too many to ask for, he asked his companion. They went home and made a list of the towns requiring missionaries and the numbers needed at each, and decided that 70 were not too many. A small group went to prayer, and then Hudson sent a telegram to Benjamin: 'RECEIVE AND SEND OUT 42 MEN AND 28 WOMEN.'

The General Secretary was surprised to receive these instructions. This meant, in addition to his already full programme, another exacting round of letter writing, interviewing, training, accommodating and despatching, tasks which he shared with his assistant, J.E. Cardwell. Very soon applications began to pour in in response to the news of the appeal for the 'Seventy'. Imagine Benjamin's shock and surprise when 22 year old Gertrude and 21 year old Hudson (now working at the Stock Exchange) one after the other knocked at his office door to ask to be included in this appeal. They had both been attending the mission prayer meetings and heard talks from returning missionaries, but their response at such tender ages was quite unexpected.

Amelia secretly wept over this family development with a mixture of pride and grief. Since their removal to Pyrland Road her children had been reared in a strong missionary atmosphere, and in their family prayers she had taught them to pray for the workers in faraway China. But the thought of the youthful Gertrude and Hudson going across the world to face all the known hazards of life in the interior of China became a burden which she quietly laid at her Lord's feet.

The peripatetic Hudson Taylor arrived in London in March, 1883. He observed with relief and satisfaction in the weeks which followed that the mission was now held in high esteem by the Christian public, and that the running of the headquarters was at last going smoothly. Benjamin's enthusiastic and dedicated work was bearing fruit. In fact Hudson had hardly unpacked his luggage when his brother-in-law handed him a list of churches and groups where he was to speak. Hudson returned from these visits with not only generous cash donations for the work, but with jewels, watches and rings given to him in meetings in large private homes.

When the day came, 24 September 1884, for Gertrude and

Hudson to sail for China, Amelia went about her work at Pyrland Road with swollen eyes and heavy spirit. Whenever a break came in her duties of planning the meals and supervising the house staff she slipped away to her bedroom to share her burden with her Lord. The load was gently lifted from her, and she returned to her daily work at peace.

Within a few weeks after the departure of the two young people, the appeal for 'Seventy' had been successful, the number even having been exceeded. They had gone out in batches as and when their training was complete. Once again the faith of Hudson Taylor had been vindicated.

Wave after wave — first the 'Eighteen', then the 'Seventy'. Next came the 'Cambridge Seven'. This latter whirlwind event, which swept the churches and universities of Britain, is described separately in chapter 10 — crowded meetings, enthusiastic press reports and hurried behind-the-scenes organisation. The outcome was clearly that the humble and despised China Inland Mission, long criticised for the poorly educated workers which it had recruited, suddenly rode on a tide of popularity as these seven young men, bursting with evangelical zeal, took the country by storm as they spoke to eager crowds of their call by God to a life of service in China.

This crowded month of meetings up and down the country brought Benjamin to the most exciting and rewarding period in his life. It revealed his genius for organising and his obvious flair in public relations.

In the wake of these countrywide meetings came a flood of applications for service, and among them many from university graduates, the kind of workers urgently needed to master the difficult Chinese language and to present Christ to the scholars and leaders of the Central Kingdom.

Eighteen months after the spectacular recruitment and departure of the 'Cambridge Seven' Benjamin received a cable from

Hudson Taylor in China — 'BANDED PRAYER. NEXT YEAR ONE HUNDRED NEW WORKERS TO BE SENT. PLEASE ACT AS SOON AS POSSIBLE.' He replied in a letter soon afterwards, 'As to The Hundred desired, we shall rejoice if a hundred of the right type are forthcoming.' There was both caution and a spirit of co-operation in these words.

Then followed a cable from Shanghai saying that Hudson was coming to Britain. It is impossible for us to realise how tiring these frequent journeys to Britain by Hudson Taylor must have been for him, but the founder was determined to achieve his latest goal in recruitment. When Benjamin received this cable he characteristically again sprang into action — another band of new recruits was needed. Hudson arrived in early 1887 to find that there was a long list of appointments to speak in churches and other gatherings waiting for him.

Everywhere the mission leader went there was an enthusiastic response to his appeal for more workers. In Edinburgh and Glasgow there were many university students to be interviewed. Back in London Benjamin was burning the midnight oil handling a pile of letters from applicants, arranging for interviews, going through all the familiar steps until candidates were bid farewell by their local churches.

By November 1887 the 'Hundred' appeal had reached 102. The workers were going out in batches. On 26 January 1888 their twenty year old Edith was among those who sailed for China. The previous year their son Marshall had gone to Cambridge University. He had expressed the wish to use his gifts of writing for the work of the mission. One by one the children were not only leaving the nest but embarking on a dangerous life in the interior of China.

In October 1890, Marshall, following on his graduation, sailed for China on the S.S. *Shannon*. The departure of their fourth child was as painful to Amelia as that of the three previous ones. Marshall says that she could not go to the docks to see him off, she could not even bid him farewell in the hall. 'She sank upon the stairs, and there the parting took place.' Amelia did not only grieve, 'she rejoiced, for nothing gave her greater joy than giving up for Christ, or to see her children walking in the truth'.

All four children — Gertrude, Hudson, Edith and Marshall — were designated to work in Taiyuan, Shanxi. In 1892 word reached Benjamin and Amelia that Edith, Hudson and Marshall were all weak with typhus. A strange peace came over the troubled parents as they prayed earnestly for them:

> Peace, perfect peace, with loved ones far away?
> In Jesus' keeping we are safe, and they.

All three missionaries recovered and resumed their work.

Included in Benjamin's job description in 1875 was 'assistance in the production of the *China's Millions*. Later, when he had proved his competence in this field, he became the fully-fledged Editor, though this was not printed as such in the magazine.

Hudson Taylor was a skilled communicator, and in founding a society which was not attached to any home denomination, was aware of the important principle that 'every number must have a cutting edge'. With this sense of perspective he personally supervised and checked every page of the magazine before its publication. Whether he was travelling in a crowded boat going up the Yangzi or visiting a faraway station in inland China, he would diligently go through the draft of the forthcoming issue before sending it back to London.

Another basic principle which he followed was 'Only sell success' — a phrase which has a modern ring about it. In the context of the *China's Millions* it meant omitting any references to set-backs and dismissals. It was important to show to the mission supporters in Britain that the mission was making progress in its programme of evangelizing China.

For some years an *Occasional Paper* had been sent to the home supporters. Its final issue was dated March 1875. One of the reasons for bringing Benjamin into the work was to enlist his help in the production of a new magazine and ultimately to make him its editor. Thus the first issue was dated July 1875. Hudson Taylor designed an attractive format with the Biblical names 'Ebenezer' and 'Jehovah Jireh' in Chinese characters above the title 'China's Millions'.

Initially Benjamin concentrated on choosing suitable extracts from missionaries' reports and letters describing their work and their travels. Soon an Editorial became a regular feature. At the back of the magazine all donations were acknowledged under Receipt Number, and Amount. In this way a donor could identify his contribution whilst remaining anonymous. Over the years certain features were included at regular times — articles with photos explaining Chinese customs and culture, the growth of the Chinese churches, news about any disasters, crises or problems — opium smoking, famine, drought, floods. There was regular reference to the work of other societies in China; and from time to time Hudson Taylor would make a statement about the mission's developing plans and strategy.

Benjamin's extensive reading enabled him to make reference to the wider missionary movement in the world. He liked to refer to past missionary heroes — the work of Adoniram Judson in Burma, the travels of David Livingstone in Africa. Benjamin and Hudson worked well together (though sometimes Hudson had to rebuke his brother-in-law for lack of promptness in sending him the material) on this important aspect of the mission's witness, so that *China's Millions* had a large and wide readership. Politicians and government leaders subscribed to it, for it gave much needed information about political events in China.

———————

We have seen that Benjamin Broomhall was successful in publicising the work of the CIM through the addresses which he gave, and through the sending out of missionaries who were home on furlough to speak at the various churches. We have seen how careful he was to acknowledge donations, both large and small, received from the mission's supporters. We have described the enthusiastic response which Benjamin and Amelia gave to the appeals for more workers, and their handling of so many groups of new recruits for China; how he organised large gatherings to send off the 'Cambridge Seven', and wrote a book about them which was widely read and had an influence beyond the work of the CIM. In a later chapter we will note the important role which Benjamin played for his mission in ending the scandal of Britain's opium trade.

His work was many-faceted. With his gift of tact and diplomacy he was an able reconciler. Marshall, his son, recalls that when there were disagreements among the large family of children, father would be called upon to arbitrate and his verdict was unanimously accepted. He also said, 'With him [Benjamin] any misrepresentation, any untruthfulness, anything unfair, was sure to be lovingly but sternly rebuked and possibly severely punished.'

There was the gift of letter writing. Benjamin Broomhall did not find it easy to dictate letters to a secretary, but preferred to write in his own free-flowing and elegant handwriting. He conducted an extensive correspondence across the world, and formed many friendships through using this natural gift which he had. He wrote to humble artisans who had given sacrificially to the work of the mission, as well as to people in high society involved in the causes which he supported. He sometimes wrote letters which were four pages in length.

These letters became an inspiration and blessing to many. The Rev. Samuel Chadwick, later President of the Wesleyan Methodist Conference, wrote to Benjamin, 'I have almost begun to look to your letters for spiritual comfort and counsel in most things that I undertake.' Charles Haddon Spurgeon, in the thick of the 'Downgrade Controversy' in the Baptist Union, likewise wrote, 'I have been horribly depressed, and like David at Ziklag have had to encourage myself in the Lord. Oh, how good He is! I had died if He had not succoured me. Peace be to you and thanks for your good word. My brother, you have refreshed me. God bless you.' As Benjamin was a regular reader of Spurgeon's sermons and had a great admiration for this Baptist preacher, this compliment must have been encouraging.

In the sphere of relationships between one missionary and another, between the China Council and individual missionaries, between the mission and the Christian public, Benjamin excelled himself as a mediator. Sometimes parents of new candidates were critical of the treatment which their young people had received from the London Council or reluctant for their young person to go to the mission field. Hudson Taylor used to say, 'I do not know of any man in the world who is more likely to help than my good brother-in-law.' Benjamin would meet the parents and the problem would be amicably solved.

Then there was his ability to communicate with the national leaders in Parliament and the churches. Dr. James Maxwell, his close friend and colleague in the Anti-Opium fight, said of Benjamin,[1]

> He loved to bring men together in large social conferences. His breakfast gatherings, first in the Exeter Hall and later in the Cecil Hotel, and other places, were a real strength to the [anti-opium] movement. They brought together leading men in the churches and members of Parliament and influential laymen. They might be expensive, but Mr. Broomhall was so trusted by wealthy Christian men who were themselves interested in the anti-opium crusade, that whenever he judged that the right time had come for such a social conference, the funds were always ready.

Dr. Eugene Stock of the Church Missionary Society wrote to Benjamin, 'I quite think you are the one to influence the big men. There is a knack in these things, and you have it.' Benjamin used that knack on many occasions.

Finally there was Benjamin's deep concern for the underdog. It was no doubt due to the example given by his father, Charles Broomhall, in his boyhood days in Bradley. Benjamin observed the way his father treated his farm-hands and gave them above average wages. Benjamin gave 20 years of his life opposing the slave trade, and then many more years fighting on behalf of the millions of opium addicts in China, whose lives had been ravaged by this harmful drug. Marshall said of his father:[2]

The sufferings of humanity and his strong sense of justice made him the passionate denouncer of the iniquitous opium traffic, and the fearless advocate of national righteousness. ... Parliamentary blue books and papers were accumulated for his anti-opium crusade. ... He trembled lest the judgments of God might fall upon his beloved country because of the wrongs she had done to China.

It was in the early 1890s, just before his retirement, that Benjamin had a sharp disagreement with his brother-in-law. Henry Frost of Toronto was pressing Hudson Taylor for the formation of a North American Council. Benjamin argued that Americans and Britishers do not work well together, and feared that there would be lack of cohesion by the setting up of another council. Most of the London Council supported him in this. Hudson Taylor, on a visit to Toronto, found himself carried along by the enthusiasm of young Canadians and Americans to form a branch of the CIM there. He wrote back to Benjamin appealingly, 'You don't understand what has happened here. Had you been present in the enthusiastic meetings which I attended you would think quite differently.' Happily, the disagreement was resolved. The CIM became an international mission. To the formation of the North American Council were soon added councils in Australia, Scandinavia and Germany.

Behind all this whirlwind of activity was a man who was loyal to his family, regular in his writing of letters to them and systematic in his praying for everyone with whom he lived and worked, as well as for the work of God throughout the world. After Benjamin's death one of his sons found two pieces of paper in his office, written in the days of his youth, which revealed the habits on which he had built his life. He wrote: 'Write regularly to Father and Mother, and Charles, William, Edwin, John, Samuel, James — to each, say, once a month. I desire one in return each month from each, excepting Samuel and James' [then too young].

On the next sheet the following words were added: 'Make it a rule to pray for the following persons'. He then recorded the names of the family mentioned above, and then the names of 36 others. 'Each person connected with the house of business, including porters and servants. ... the YMCA; the success of missionary labourers; the Church of Christ Universal; ... the sections of the Church in this country — Church of England, Wesleyan, Independent, Baptist etc.'

One of the tributes paid to Benjamin after his death was, 'So much influence has seldom been combined with so little prominence, as in the life of Benjamin Broomhall.' Today Hudson Taylor is a household name in Christian circles, but little is known of his brother-in-law, without whose service the rapid growth of the mission in this period would never have been achieved. And Benjamin would not have wanted it to be otherwise.

And what of Amelia, Benjamin's devoted wife? Mrs. Howard Taylor said of Amelia, 'Her hooded candle was always alight at 5 a.m., and before turning even in thought to the claims of the busy day ahead her own soul was cleansed, refreshed and renewed in fellowship with God.'

The value of Amelia's ministry of prayer and humble service behind the scenes at Pyrland Road, out of the limelight of the mission's public activities, was incalculable. Her utter devotion to her brother Hudson as he faced physical dangers, acute illness in China and severe criticism at home remained undiminished, although she sometimes inwardly felt that he was foolhardy in such matters as the wearing of Chinese clothes.

Marshall's brief biography reveals the deep love and fidelity which Amelia had for Benjamin. She stood faithfully by him both during the difficult years in the drapery business and in his busy public life in the work of the CIM. Her spiritual influence on the candidates going to China was inestimable, and her unselfish bringing up of her large family of ten, together with the seven children of Hudson, bore much fruit in their later lives. Marshall says: 'Throughout the history of the mission there was no improvement, development or special difficulty, of which she was cognisant, but she set herself to pray a way through. As she had, with a sister's love, interceded for her pioneer brother in China when he first went forth alone, so she interceded for the work of God as it grew.'

Phyllis Thompson says of Amelia, 'She never went to China, performed no acts of outstanding courage, had no spectacular achievements to her credit, swayed no audiences with eloquence ... But without the Amelias there would be no mission.'

Notes

1. B. Broomhall, *National Righteousness*, Aug. 1911, p. 8.
2. M. Broomhall, *Heirs Together*, pp. 105, 106.

10

An unexpected breakthrough

On a wet winter's night in 1885 hundreds of Londoners were converging on the Exeter Hall in the Strand — some in dignified carriages and cabs, while others had been walking from the East End slums. Into the spacious hall crowded titled lords and ladies in their finery, smart businessmen, humble shop assistants, labourers — all eager to obtain seats in the much publicised gathering.

On the platform at the front were seated 40 Cambridge undergraduates, and behind them hung a spacious map of the Chinese Empire. As the clock struck the hour the Chairman, George Williams, entered, followed by seven distinguished-looking young men. They were known as men of high social standing and some of athletic achievement. A hush came over the crowded hall as the people looked in admiration at the young men who had become household names in recent weeks.

There was a full programme, and the opening addresses were short and to the point. Williams, Treasurer of the fast growing YMCA, appealed for prayerful support for the CIM, the only interdenominational society working in China. Benjamin, as Secretary of the mission, spoke of the service which the mission was rendering to the other societies working in China in the form of making maps, supplying information and publicity about missionary work there. Robert Landale, an Oxford graduate and a missionary on furlough, told how nine years previously while a law student he had heard God's call to work in China. It was a lonely and misunderstood life, but abundantly worthwhile, he testified.

Then the young men who came to be called the 'Cambridge Seven' addressed the gathering. There was Stanley Smith, former Cambridge rowing stroke, Montagu Beauchamp, a baronet's son, D.E. Hoste, a gunner subaltern and son of a Major-General, W.W. Cassels of Repton and St. John's, a Church of England curate (later a bishop), Cecil Polhill-Turner of the Dragoon guards, his brother Arthur of Eton and Trinity Hall, and C.T. Studd of Eton and Cambridge, a brilliant cricketer.

They had all been converted through the fruitful ministry in Britain of American evangelist, D.L. Moody, five of them through his Cambridge mission. They spoke of God's call to them to leave everything to serve him in faraway China, and challenged the audience to a similar dedication. Some went to the Lower Hall to speak to those who could not hear the main addresses. The meeting went on for several hours, but the close attention of the listeners never abated.

The meeting on 4 February was the climax of a series of meetings throughout the country in the previous weeks in Liverpool, Aberdeen, Edinburgh, Glasgow, Greenock, Newcastle, Leeds, Rochdale, Manchester, Bristol, Oxford and Cambridge. Wherever they went they addressed crowded meetings. Dozens responded to their appeal for commitment to Christ, as well as to service for God on the mission fields.

The next morning the 'Cambridge Seven' were bidden farewell at Victoria Station. At ten o'clock the boat train took them on the first lap of their six week journey.

In that month of special gatherings throughout Britain, the China Inland Mission was suddenly lifted in a blaze of publicity from being a 'mission of cranks' to one of prominence and great respect. Up to now the recruits for China had been artisans and people of limited education. The tide had clearly turned.

But it also proved to be a high point for all Protestant

missions. The *Nonconformist* commented, 'Never before, prob-
ably, in the history of missions has so unique a band set out to
labour in the foreign field as the one which stood last night on
the platform of Exeter Hall; and rarely has more enthusiasm
been evoked than was aroused by their appearance and their
stirring words'. The missionary cause became a talking point
among Christians of all the denominations. Eugene Stock, the
historian of the Church Missionary Society, was to describe the
years 1885, 1886 and 1887 as 'The Three Memorable Years.'
Candidates joined the CMS in record numbers. Baptist, Presbyterian and Methodist missions likewise had a burst of applications for missionary work.

Behind all these exciting developments the self-effacing
Benjamin Broomhall had played an important role. He had
personally arranged the meetings at the Colston Hall in Bristol,
the Guild Hall in Cambridge, the Corn Exchange in Oxford and
the Exeter Hall in London; and had spoken at most of them. In
faith he had committed the mission to the expenses of hiring
these large buildings, and this decision had been abundantly
vindicated. The offerings had covered the costs.

The YMCA leaders who had booked the Exeter Hall in
London had had 'cold feet' five days before the meeting was
due, but Broomhall had assumed responsibility for the mission's
expenses, a decision which was subsequently fully justified. He
later said of the Exeter Hall gathering, 'I question if a meeting of
equal significance and spiritual fruitfulness has been held in that
building during this generation. Its influence upon the cause of
missions must be immense, incalculable ... The Exeter Hall was
packed in every part, and people of note and title had to get in
anywhere and be thankful if they got in at all.'

But for Benjamin the hard work did not stop with the departure
of the seven young men. Letters poured in for information about
the mission. There were donations for the work in inland China,
applications for service with the CIM and requests for speakers
at various churches. He burned the midnight oil answering the
flood of correspondence in his own flowing hand, and spent many
busy hours completing the necessary arrangements.

Chira Inland Mission.

2. 4 & 6. *Pyrland Road, Mildmay.*

London, Oct 26ᵈ 1886
N.

To the Queen's Most Excellent Majesty

Madam,

Permit me very humbly to ask your
Majesty's acceptance of the accompanying volume,
"A Missionary Band".

It contains a record of some deeply interesting
particulars concerning a band of Young Men,
two of whom resigned their Commissions in Your
Majesty's Army in order to devote their lives to the
work of Christian Missionaries in China, another
of them was one of the foremost gentleman Cricketers of
England, while another was an oar, Stroke - oar of
the Cambridge boat in the University boat race

The second part of the book sets forth in the words
of many distinguished men (not a few of them among
the brightest ornaments of Your Majesty's reign) the
supreme importance of the work of making the Gospel
known in Heathen and Mahommedan lands; and of
all the bright pages in the history of the period covered
by your Majesty's reign, there can be none brighter,
or which will afford more solid satisfaction to the

Your Majesty's most faithful

subject, and dutiful Servant

B Broomhall

**Part of a letter written by Benjamin Broomhall to Queen Victoria
enclosing a copy of his *A Missionary Band*.**

Fifty thousand copies of the *China's Millions* for July 1885 describing these special meetings were printed and sold out. A year later Benjamin published *A Missionary Band — a Record of Missionary Consecration*, which repeated the testimonies and addresses in the earlier *China's Millions*, but also added photographs, maps and subsequent news of the work of the 'Seven' in China. Twenty thousand were printed, and all were sold. The final version *The Evangelization of the World* was published, which had additional sections on missions in Africa and India, an indication of the ecumenical spirit of the CIM. Benjamin sent Queen Victoria a copy of the gilt-edged edition, which she accepted. Benjamin's friend, Sir George Williams, financed the sending of a copy of *The Evangelization of the World* to every YMCA branch in Britain.

The influence of this book spread across the seas. Robert Speer, Secretary of American Presbyterian missions, stated that apart from the Bible no books had so influenced his life of dedication to the cause of missions as Blaikie's *Personal Life of Livingstone* and Broomhall's *The Evangelization of the World*. World missionary statesman Dr. John R. Mott testified to the influence of this book on his own life. Two years later the title of Broomhall's book became part of the motto of the Student Volunteer Movement — 'the evangelization of the world in this generation'.

The unique success of the 'Cambridge Seven' meetings and subsequent publications revealed Benjamin Broomhall's abilities and skills in publicity and public relations. Forty new missionaries joined the mission in 1885, the year when the seven young men departed for China. Behind the acceptance of each candidate was some months of corresponding, at least one interview, training and preparation at the mission home. The home itself was uncomfortably crowded with the arrivals and departures of workers, and this placed further pressure on Amelia as the matron and mother of the centre.

Benjamin with his sensitive spirit, though excited and encouraged by all that had happened in January and February 1885, felt constrained to warn, 'The hour of success is often the time of danger.' The undoubted gains of the year had to be marshalled with a cautious optimism.

The dramatic story of the recruitment of the 'Cambridge Seven' did not end when they boarded the boat train at Victoria Station. Behind them in Britain the momentum of their meetings was being maintained.

From Edinburgh Professor Henry Drummond was organising evangelistic and revival meetings across Scotland, with professors and lecturers taking part. At Cambridge, Handley Moule, Principal of Ridley Hall was finding that the enthusiasm among his theological students for going to the mission field was such that he had to make appeals for the work of the ministry at home. In the USA C.T. Studd's brother, John, was pressing home his brother's appeal for the missions. Benjamin's book, *A Missionary Band*, led directly to the formation in 1886 of the Student Volunteer Missionary Union. In 1891 Robert Wilder came to Britain and formed the SVMU there. From this body the British SCM and IVF were eventually born.

Benjamin Broomhall was now at the peak of his ministry as an advocate of missionary work. Having bidden farewell to the seven young men, he must have wondered whether, after all the excitement and crowds surrounding their departure for China, the bubble might burst and their unbounded enthusiasm come to nought.

At the time of the departure of the 'Cambridge Seven,' Robert Wilder had written in *The Missionary Review*: 'Thoughtful minds will be waiting to see how the glow of their piety endures the tug and toil of learning the Chinese language, and then close contact daily with the masses of ignorant and superstitious idolaters, with no bracing influences around them from cultured Christian society.'

Benjamin's thoughts must have been very similar. In the months and years which lay ahead he followed their experiences with prayerful interest. Letters and reports trickled in to his London office, and extracts from them were published initially in his best selling book *The Evangelization of the World*, and subsequently in *China's Millions*.

The party of young men travelled to Dover, Calais, Brindisi, Suez, Colombo and Hong Kong. Clearly, after the crowded meetings and travel throughout Britain, they were entitled to have a rest on the voyage, in order to be fresh for the language study and journeyings into the interior of China, which lay ahead. But their voyage to China, as reported in Benjamin's book, sounds like a chapter out of the book of Acts and the missionary journeys of St. Paul. They held services on board ship and they had personal chats with the crew and fellow travellers resulting in conversions. When ashore they spoke to church and mission school groups. One traveller later wrote in *The Indian Witness*: 'No cowards these. Calmly smiling at scornful looks, boldly they stand firm, ever ready to fight in the cause of their heavenly Master. ...'

At Hong Kong some of the 'Seven' spoke at a crowded meeting, arranged at short notice, in the City Hall Theatre, while others scattered across the colony to speak at other meetings.

After six weeks of travel they reached Shanghai where they were welcomed by Hudson Taylor himself. There they addressed the English residents, and at the first meeting the first to respond was the youthful British chaplain of the Cathedral. They went on to address large audiences at the Lyceum Theatre, the Mansion Hall and some athletic clubs. One report said, 'They have more thoroughly affected Shanghai than any series of meetings that have ever been held here.'

It was at Shanghai that the first test of their acceptance of the mission's regulations was put to the test. Their heads were shaved, and they donned pigtails and native dress. Arthur Polhill-Turner wrote home, 'It is a comfortable dress, and wonderfully suited to the climate which greatly varies.'

The group then split into two. C.T. Studd and the Polhill-Turner brothers (and with Montague Beauchamp for the first part of the journey) went up the Yangzi in their Chinese clothes. At Hankou, Griffith John, the LMS missionary, arranged for them to address the local European residents. As they continued on their journey Studd and the Polhill-Turner brothers put away their language books and prayed for a Pentecostal gift to speak Chinese. But this experiment stopped soon after they arrived at Hanzhong, and they duly resumed their studies.

The second group — Stanley Smith, Dixon Hoste and William Cassels — travelled to Shanxi via Yantai, Tianjin and Peking. At all these centres they had successful meetings with missionaries of all societies. Stanley Smith, a fervent preacher and orator, moved the missionaries with his appeal for rededication to the work they had been called to do. The Rev. Dr. Joseph Edkins of the LMS in Peking wrote afterwards: 'Such meetings I have never known in China. I take it as a sign that the revival waves are now beating on the China shore. ...'

In the Peking meetings 25 missionaries signed a joint letter to missions everywhere, testifying to the impact of the addresses given by the recently arrived young men. The letter ended with the appeal: 'If we would all unite, have we not faith to believe that God would shake China with His power?'

Travelling from Tianjin to Peking, and then from the capital city to their destination in Taiyuan, Shanxi, this group had their first experience of conditions in China. William Cassels wrote: 'We have had our first experience of cart travelling and of Chinese inns. The shaking up of the former did us a lot of good physically, and made the shaking down in the latter all the more welcome when night comes on. As to the inns, I must say we found them exceedingly comfortable.'

Soon the seven new recruits in inland China had to leave behind memories of crowded meetings in Britain and China, and get down to the discipline of language study and the inevitable problems of winning converts and building small churches in a land very resistant to the Gospel.

Benjamin Broomhall, back in London, followed their work with prayer and fatherly concern. He made regular reference to them in his reports in *China's Millions*. Clearly neither he nor the CIM would ever be quite the same again.

We now look at the work of the 'Seven' during the rest of their lives. John Pollock rightly states, 'Not one of the "Cambridge Seven" looked back, though their paths widely diverged.'

William Cassels, the eldest of them, proved to be an effective pastor to his Chinese flock. After a year in Shanxi he was transferred to Sichuan, where he could carry on his work with good Anglican orderliness. Hudson Taylor planned that eastern Sichuan should be run on Church of England principles, and so here a diocese was formed jointly by the CIM and the CMS. Cassels, the first ordained Anglican clergyman to join the CIM, was ordained Bishop of Western China in 1895 and served at the Baoning Cathedral for thirty years till his death.

Stanley Smith worked exclusively in Shanxi province. Differing in later years doctrinally with the Shanghai Council, in that he believed in 'conditional immortality', he opened a small mission in eastern Shanxi, where he died in 1931.

C.T. Studd, the popular cricketer, worked faithfully in Shanxi and Shaanxi before experiencing poor health. He was invalided home in 1894, but never lost his missionary vision. He worked as pastor of a church in India, and then at the age of fifty Studd set off into tropical Africa. He founded the Heart of Africa Mission, which later became the Worldwide Evangelistic Crusade. Studd died at Ibambi in Zaire in 1931.

Arthur Polhill-Turner, who had commenced studies for the Anglican ministry when in Britain, worked at Bazhong and Baoning in the Sichuan Anglican diocese, where he was ordained in 1888. He retired from his work in China in 1928, and served a Hertfordshire church for the last seven years of his life. His brother, Cecil, worked in Gansu and Sichuan. With a special burden for the evangelisation of Tibet, he approached this forbidden land both from the China and the India sides, facing many physical dangers. He founded the Tibetan Pioneer Band. Cecil was invalided home in 1900, but with his evangelistic fervour for the work in China, made seven prolonged visits back to the interior of the country, dying in Britain in 1938, aged eighty.

Of the 'Seven', Montagu Beauchamp was the successful itinerant worker, taking long evangelistic journeys, sometimes in company with Hudson Taylor, in north-west and south-west China; and latterly assisted Cassels as a lay worker in Baoning. He returned to Britain in 1911 and was ordained. He revisited China three times, visiting his son who was working in Baoning. He died in Langzhong, Sichuan, in 1939 during his third visit.

Dixon Hoste worked in Shanxi with Pastor Xi (see chapter 12), and in 1903 succeeded Hudson Taylor as the General Director of the mission, retiring in 1935. After internment by the Japanese in Shanghai, he died in London in 1946.

In retrospect the story of the 'Cambridge Seven' and their evangelistic endeavours stands as one of the great missionary events of the nineteenth century.

Picture illustrating the evil effects of opium in China.

11

Fighting the Opium Dragon

Try and imagine this strange scene. One sunny day in March, 1839, a high-ranking Chinese officer could be seen on a large boat travelling up the Pearl river towards Guangzhou. Around him was an entourage of fellow VIPs. As the boat drew nearer, the Westerners and Chinese merchants on the riverside could see the officer more clearly — he was a middle-aged man, corpulent, with a pronounced black moustache and a long beard.

Following closely behind the large boat were smaller ones with other officials on board. It was clearly to be a day of drama and ceremony, for the crews manning the boats were dressed in red and white, with rattan hats to match. Looking further afield, even the troops lined along the river edge in front of the forts were wearing bright new uniforms. Nothing like this had been seen before in these parts. Something must be about to happen.

Soon the mystery was resolved. The high-ranking officer was the new Commissioner, Lin Zexu. He had been commissioned by none other than the Emperor, the 'Son of Heaven', to wipe out the dreaded opium trade completely from the Central Kingdom, lock, stock and barrel. For more than half a century the opium traders had defied the laws of the Empire, and thrust their vessels, laden with opium, up the Pearl river and up the China coast. The undeniable fact was that scholars, merchants and peasants alike had become addicts, many of them reduced to skin and bones, to debt and starvation.

Lin spent eight days carefully investigating the many aspects of the nefarious trade. Detailed questions were asked of the compradors, of the factories and of the hong merchants.[1] Then, after close consultation with his officials, his mind was made up as to what must be done. The barbarians must hand over to him every grain of opium on their boats and in their warehouses, and solemnly promise never again to force opium on his people. To the surprised merchants he announced there was to be no more opium trading or smuggling, and, if there was, the death penalty would ensue.

A new broom sweeps clean. Lin really meant business. The British must hand over all opium under their control by the 24 March 1839, or the Chinese brokers would be executed. He blockaded the factory by land and sea, thus imprisoning the British traders and merchants. Captain Charles Elliott, Chief Superintendent of British trade, having both to save lives and avoid damage to British property, acted promptly and arranged for the surrender of 20,283 chests of opium, and made an undertaking that his merchants would stop trafficking in the drug. Whereupon Lin lifted the blockade on the factory. But the opium clippers continued racing up the coast to sell their cargo.

The drastic actions of Commissioner Lin were daring and carefully planned. It was a desperate strategy aimed at bringing to an end the humiliation and degradation caused by the opium trade, which had been thrust on a nation proud of its history and culture. The Emperor was relying on this new appointee to solve this prolonged and harmful problem once and for all.

But, to Britain's shame, the trade continued. Two and a half years after the colourful drama which I have described took place, Captain Elliott had another plan. Subjects of Her Majesty had been treated unjustly and violently, they had been blockaded and imprisoned. And so he led an expedition of heavily armed ships to as far north as the Beihe.

To the Emperor such an advance, to so close to Peking, was humiliating and indicative of failure by Lin to control the opium traders. He promptly fired Lin, and sent him into exile to far away Xinjiang. That was the end of the man who had signally shown such courage and vision. History has, however, given a different verdict. To this day Lin Zexu is remembered as a national hero.

The opium had not gone away. Soon after these events two Opium Wars followed, from 1840 to 1843, and in 1856. The scale of opium smuggling and trading continued to increase, and land which had produced grain was now planted with the opium poppy. Schooners and brigs continued to cut their determined way through typhoons and pirate-infested waters to every open port in China.

The public in Britain appeared to have no idea of the damage the trade was doing to the Chinese people. Some news trickled through from time to time which suggested the problem had assumed dangerous proportions. Baron Richtofen, a geographer travelling through Henan and Shanxi in north China, reported seeing 'whole towns disfigured by haggard faces and staring eyes, consequent upon the use of opium'.

It took a long time for protests to be made by the British people about the harm the opium trade was doing in China. Christians were the first to take action. Letters and speeches by Hudson Taylor used the strongest language to portray the tragic effects of opium addiction. Evangelicals and Quakers began to see the opium trade as an obstacle to the progress of Christianity in China. As already stated, in 1843 Lord Shaftesbury had challenged the opium monopoly in a speech in the House of Commons. Missionary societies working in China joined in the protest with petitions signed by thousands of mission supporters. The anti-opium lobby was becoming more organised and more articulate.

A committee was formed in 1874 which became the Anglo-Oriental Society for the Suppression of the Opium Trade. It received generous funding from Sir Edward Pease, a Quaker baronet from Yorkshire, who became the society's president. They launched *The Friend of China* as their official magazine.

It was at this stage that Benjamin Broomhall entered the fight against opium. Since becoming the General Secretary of the CIM in 1878 and subsequently the Editor of *China's Millions*, he had begun to follow his brother-in-law, Hudson Taylor, into the fight against the opium traffic. In every issue of the magazine there were articles from the pen of Hudson Taylor, as well as excerpts from reports by missionaries on the field on the tragic effects of the trade.

The attack by concerned Christians was gathering momentum. In April 1881, an Anti-Opium Conference was held at Mildmay, near the CIM's headquarters. At it Lord Shaftesbury, Benjamin's old friend from the anti-slavery days, described the opium traffic as 'the greatest of modern abominations since the slave trade'. That autumn a similar gathering was held in Mansion House with a wider range of support. On the platform were the Archbishop of Canterbury, Cardinal Manning and Lord Shaftesbury. These meetings spilled over into the House of Commons in heated debates in the years which followed. The leading champion was the Quaker baronet, Sir John Pease.

The tempo was increasing. In 1882 there was a united meeting of missionaries held in the Exeter Hall on the subject of 'The Truth about Opium Smoking'. When the meetings were over Benjamin put together speeches and quotations from the addresses into a booklet under the same title. In 1883 the *China's Millions* ran a series of articles on the production of opium in India and its harm to China. By now Benjamin, in his capacity as the General Secretary of the CIM with its large work in China, was on the Executive Committee of the Society for the Suppression of the Opium Trade. He was taking up the anti-opium cause with the enthusiasm and drive which he applied to any worthy cause which fired his imagination. He addressed meetings and joined a delegation to speak to Lord Gladstone on the manufacture of opium in India.

The next great opportunity to influence public opinion on the opium trade was the Third International Missionary Conference of 1888, which met in the Exeter Hall under the presidency of the Earl of Aberdeen. To it came 1,579 delegates representing

128 missionary societies. Benjamin was on the Executive Committee of this important body, and it was while on this committee that he met and formed a close friendship with a fellow member, Dr. James Maxwell, an English Presbyterian missionary invalided home from Taiwan, where he had witnessed the harmful effects of opium addiction first hand. The two men were to work together closely to fight the opium trade for the subsequent 20 years.

These two committee members demanded that the conference apportion time for debating the problem of opium, but this body decided that it would not be placed on the agenda. Undeterred, the two men appealed to the General Committee, who upheld the appeal, and added an extra day to the conference. But imagine the disappointment of Broomhall and Maxwell on the final day, when they learned that the time was to be shared with two other causes.

When the day came, Hudson Taylor gave a powerful speech, drawing on his first hand experience of the effects of opium throughout China. He said: 'I have laboured in China for over thirty years, and am profoundly convinced that the opium traffic is doing more evil in China in a week than missions are doing good in a year.'

Benjamin Broomhall in a long speech, said among other things: 'The opium trade is one of the most gigantic evils that the world has ever been cursed with. I believe in my conscience that there has never been, in the history of the world, an instance in which one nation has so wronged another, as England has wronged China.'

Hudson Taylor proposed the following resolution:

That this Conference desires to put on record its sense of the incalculable evils — physical, moral and social — which continue to be wrought in China through the opium trade ... that it recognises clearly that nothing short of the entire suppression of the trade, so far as it is in the power of the Government to suppress it, can meet the claims of the case.

This was unanimously adopted by the meeting. But the next disappointment came when the conference committee ruled that this resolution did not represent the conference as a whole.

There was one aspect of the debate on opium at the conference which should not be overlooked, as it reveals a very important aspect of Benjamin's personality. While the vast majority of delegates supported the appeals for a speedy end to the opium trade, there were a few who surprisingly opposed them. Among them was Dr. R.N. Cust, an Indian Civil Service official and a delegate for the CMS. He warned that missionaries should not get involved in politics, agriculture or commerce, and used some strange arguments against taking any action: 'There are two thousand miles of sea coast, with rivers and creeks. The fleets of England, the fleets of the world, could not prevent the export of opium from India.'

Benjamin, with his strong feelings and powerful convictions about trading in opium, then gave an address which was a model of courtesy and restraint, adopting a style which was perhaps a forerunner of the twentieth century philosophy of Dale Carnegie's, *How to Win Friends and Influence People*. This is an extract of Benjamin Broomhall's remarkable reply to Dr. Cust:[2]

> Mr. Chairman, it is known to most on the platform and to many here, that my friend Dr. Cust and myself, on this question, are at points of extreme antagonism. But I wish to say in this meeting that I cherish for him feelings of warm admiration; I personally respect him for his services, and on the question of missionary work, he has devoted a long and honourable life to the study of the progress of the work of God in all lands. On questions philological, ethnological, geographical, in their relation to missions, I do not know any man whose information is so wide and so accurate. But on this point, for some strange reason that I cannot understand, he is on the wrong side. I want to tell our friend Dr. Cust, and all who think with him, that we are determined to beat them.

What a gracious approach to such a highly charged subject!

Returning to the disappointment which Broomhall and

Maxwell experienced when the conference committee ruled that the opium resolution did not represent the conference as a whole, their response was to make immediate plans to take urgent and effective action. The matter was further aggravated by their feelings in recent months that the Society for the Suppression of the Opium Trade was running out of steam. They felt that it was spending too much time on formalities and procedures. Benjamin had a strong dislike for constitutions and laws in the running of voluntary societies. When one new society was formed later, he was informed of its elaborate constitution. He told the shocked secretary of this new organisation to put the new constitution in a safe, lock it up, lose the key and forget all about it!

Six days after the Exeter Hall meetings Broomhall and Maxwell formed the Christian Union for the Severance of the British Empire with the Opium Traffic. The founders were quick to emphasize that the Christian Union would complement rather than rival the society which had been working for fourteen years. They would minimize formalities and act with urgency. And so, on 26 June 1888, the Christian Union was formed with *National Righteousness* as its official magazine. The name was based on the verse in Scripture, 'Righteousness exalteth a nation, but sin is a reproach to any people.' (Proverbs 14:34). Its president was S.A. Blackwood KCB, and Benjamin its secretary. Members were to subscribe a shilling a year, and no less than 1,600 joined immediately. Among its supporters were well-known personalities such as Dr. Thomas Barnardo, Dr. Gratton Guinness, the Rev. C.H. Spurgeon, and of course, Dr. Hudson Taylor.

In the first issue Benjamin quoted extensively from a recently published two-volumed book by Mr. Montgomery Martin, *An Enquiry into the Opium Traffic in China*. This brief quotation will suffice: 'It is impossible to peruse the official documents without acknowledging that your Majesty's subjects are engaged in the commission of a fearful crime in China; that they are actively embarking in a traffic which is destroying the lives and deteriorating the morals of thousands of our fellow creatures.'

Benjamin also quoted from the verdict of Spurgeon, 'the prince of preachers', on the trade: 'We do not believe that one person in ten really knows what the opium scandal is. ... Our Indian finances are fed by our providing for the indulgence of one of the most degrading vices into which men can fall.'

And he could always find strong words to quote from Hudson Taylor's pen: 'England is morally responsible for every ounce of opium now produced in China, as well as that imported from abroad.'

By June 1890 there were more than 3,000 members in the Christian Union. That month's issue contained a most moving appeal from Chinese Church leaders to the Churches of Great Britain: 'Our people originally are comparatively strong and healthy. But when once they acquire the opium habit they become mere weak skeletons, children and grandchildren ... We pray the Lord above will reveal Himself and help England and China to abolish this great evil.'

Who could not but be both touched and shamed at such a plea? As a result of this Benjamin sent out a letter to 45,000 ministers of the Gospel in Britain, representing the main Protestant denominations:

> In every great movement for the removal of great wrongs there is a time of long and painful labour. There comes the crisis and the crowning hour of victory for the Lord's hosts. Does it not seem that the closing stage has now arrived, and God is calling the churches of Great Britain to the final struggle of this God-defying evil?

At the same time a letter went to each member of Parliament with facts and figures about the opium trade.

The new society was hitting hard and effectively. Soon after this Maxwell became Secretary and Treasurer of the Christian Union, and Benjamin continued as Editor of *National Righteousness*. Strong support came from the Right Hon. W.E. Gladstone, MP. Membership continued to soar — by February 1893, there were 5,000 members, and by April 6,000. Benjamin retired as the General Secretary of the CIM in 1895. He was now sixty-six. But he continued his vigorous work in the Christian Union. A

plethora of meetings were arranged to fight the opium trade —
Benjamin organised Anti-Opium conferences, public meetings
in the Exeter Hall at the Strand, breakfast meetings attended by
titled people and parliamentarians, at which he spoke with
vigour. He visited churches up and down the land, stirring up
Christians to take the opium problem seriously. Two leading
churchmen gave him their valued support — Handley Moule,
now Bishop of Durham, and Prebendary Webb-Peploe of
St. Paul's Church, Onslow Square, London.

The pace was clearly speeding up. The Society for the
Suppression of the Opium Trade and its magazine, *The Friend of
China*, the christian Union and its magazine *National Righteousness*, the CIM and its periodical *China's Millions*, all kept up the
pressure. Thousands of Wesleyan Methodists signed an urgent
petition on opium. Five thousand medical men in Britain signed
a statement that opium should be classed as a poison in India
(as it already was in Britain) and that its manufacture and sale
be prohibited other than for medicinal purposes. And in China
itself a new generation, as part of the new thinking in the years
following the Boxer Rising, was demanding an urgent end to the
harmful trade.

China took the first radical step. In 1906 an imperial decree
ruled that the importation of opium be phased out in ten years
and all land planted with the opium poppy be converted to grain
over a similar period. This action in China synchronized with
the rising pressure being applied in Britain by the fast-growing
anti-opium lobby. The British government then likewise agreed
to phase out its Indian exports over a ten-year period.

At the great Edinburgh Missionary Conference of 1910,
chaired by Dr. John R. Mott, reference was made to the 'sinister
and sordid story of the opium trade in China'. W.H.T. Gairdner,
in his record of these large gatherings, says, 'The Conference was
given reason to hope that the stain [the opium trade] is soon to
be removed.' This was strengthened by the fact that Bishop
Brent of the Philippines was going direct from this conference
to one on opium at The Hague 'for considering the means
towards an end'.

The Archbishop of York gave an address at the conference in which he said:[3]

> Can we reflect, we of the British race, without shame, upon the fact that we made wars, we extorted treaties, in order that, for our commercial advantage, we should force on a non-Christian race the purchase of a drug which was ruining its moral character? Could there be anything more prejudicial to the credit of Christianity in the eyes of the world than this, that when a non-Christian race shows itself eager to liberate itself from a moral curse, a Christian nation should be backward in co-operating with its desires?

A Commission on social issues made the following report on the evils of the opium trade:[4]

> The Commission believes that they represent the feeling of missionaries and supporters of missions in recording that (i) their conviction that the traffic in opium should cease; (ii) their regret that the history of this traffic in China has brought discredit upon Christian missions by the associating of them in the Chinese mind through the action of some Western governments in the spread of opium; (iii) their sympathy with the Chinese government in the steps at present being taken to restrict the use of opium; (iv) their hope that the British Government will act in full harmony with the Chinese Government; (v) their hope that the British Imperial and Indian governments may be able to meet the financial difficulties created by the cessation of the opium revenue in a way which shall not increase the taxing of the mass of the people in India, nor injure the Feudatory States concerned.

The anti-opium campaign was drawing wider and wider support. Success was now in sight.

Finally on 8 May 1911, Britain agreed to end all exports by 1917. Benjamin died on 29 May, but Marshall was able to read this good news to him on his deathbed. He summoned the strength to exclaim, 'A great victory. Thank God I have lived to see it.'

The articles by Dr. G.G. Morrison in *The Times* attributed this to three factors:

i the resolution passed at the 1910 Edinburgh Conference (in response to Benjamin Broomhall's strong pressure);

ii the Day of National Humiliation and Prayer arranged for 24 October 1910;

iii the bold decrees of the Chinese National Assembly in 1906.

On 7 May 1913, two years after Benjamin's death, the British Government announced, 'We are in the satisfactory position of saying that the opium trade is dead.'

Notes

1. 'Compradors' = buyers (from Portuguese);
   'Factories' = the quarters of the merchants, who were known as 'Factors';
   'Hong merchants' = a guild of Chinese merchants.
2. J. Johnston, *Centenary Conference of Protestant Missions 1888*, (London, James Nisbett, 1889), p. 133.
3. *World Missionary Conference 1910*, (Edinburgh, Oliphant, Anderson & Ferrier, 1911) Volume 9, p. 275.
4. Ibid., volume 7, pp. 164, 165.

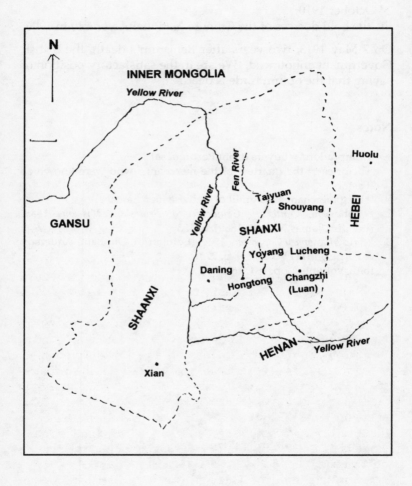

Map showing the area in north west China where the five children of Benjamin Broomhall initially worked.

12

Your Sons and your Daughters shall prophesy

Though Benjamin and Amelia never set foot in China, five of their ten children were to go out and serve God in that faraway land. From their earliest years they had heard all about missionary work in China, and the need for new workers. They had met the candidates preparing to depart, as well as the missionaries coming home on furlough. With many of these they had laughed and played. At mealtimes they overheard much news about the work in China, and sometimes they slipped into the regular prayer meetings. They certainly picked up the sense of urgency for the evangelization of China.

Little is known about how the call of God came to these sons and daughters of Benjamin and Amelia. Doubtless it came through the spiritual environment in which they were reared, the sermons and talks they heard week after week, the dispatching of the young men and women, whom they had grown to love, as they left for service in inland China and perhaps most of all, the family prayers which they had with their mother, as they heard her pray for the needs of Uncle Hudson and the other workers by name. China must be evangelized and they had to do their share.

An insight into the longings which Amelia had for her children when they were still young is given in a brief autobiographical booklet which she wrote in those early days: 'My chief desire is that you may grow up to be real followers of Christ, not mere professors of Him ... My dear children, take Him for your Friend, your Counsellor, your Guide. Tell Him all your hopes, your fears, your sorrows; be assured that He is interested in all that concerns you.'

That desire that they should grow up to be true followers of Christ was surely fulfilled. All the five young people who became missionaries were to serve initially in the important and distant province of Shanxi, in north-west China, though all would move on to work elsewhere. The China Inland Mission had first entered Shanxi in 1876, when north China was in the tight grip of a cruel and devastating famine. Five and a half million died in Shanxi alone, a third of its total population.

When the first pioneers, Francis James and Joshua Turner, arrived they witnessed scenes which left painful scars on their memories. In their diaries they recorded that as they walked along the roads they passed peasants with emaciated bodies, staggering along. On either side of the roads were skin and bone corpses. Feeble-looking villagers asked them to buy their girls in order to obtain money for food. They even witnessed cannibalism, with parents eating their children to survive. Funds arrived which came from the Lord Mayor of London's Special Appeal. This enabled them to distribute money for the purchase of food.

Soon after these pioneers arrived, Jennie Taylor, Hudson Taylor's second wife, arrived in Shanxi with two women workers to run an orphanage for children whose parents had died in the famine. They were the first single women missionaries to travel into the interior of China, and two of Benjamin's daughters would soon be following them.

It was clear that Hudson Taylor was determined to build a strong work in this important province. But problems arose in the missionary community here in 1881 and 1882 regarding the uniqueness of Christianity, the founder's style of leadership, as well as the question of wearing Chinese pigtails and dress. Four highly qualified couples resigned to form the Shouyang mission, which eventually became part of the Baptist Missionary Society. Then when the 'Cambridge Seven' arrived in China they were

Gertrude and Hudson Broomhall in their early work in Shanxi.

all designated to Shanxi province, though they worked largely in the southern part and some moved to other provinces later.

Hudson Taylor, undaunted by the setbacks, wanted to place new workers in the province who would be of unquestioned loyalty and orthodoxy. This no doubt explains why Benjamin's sons and daughters were sent to Taiyuan.

The first Broomhalls to arrive in China were the delicate looking and fair-haired Gertrude and the serious minded young Hudson. They sailed together on the P. & O. ship *Chusan* on 24 September 1884. In their youthful zeal they witnessed to a wine merchant, Stark, who turned to Christ and later joined the CIM.

There were two ships on the high seas carrying between them 17 members of the 'Seventy' new missionaries. Ahead of Gertrude and Hudson was seventeen year old Maria, Hudson Taylor's daughter, due to arrive in Shanghai a month before them. While the three young people were at sea, a cable reached Jennie then at Pyrland Road, which read: 'TROUBLE INLAND. IMPOSSIBLE TO FORWARD ARRIVALS. SEND NO MORE TILL WAY IS CLEAR'. The newspapers spoke of rioting in Wenzhou and of foreigners' premises being burned down.

When Jennie had read the message, she shared it with Benjamin and Amelia, quoting a sentence from Isaiah 30:15, 'In quietness and confidence shall be your strength.' Jennie sent the cable on to Hudson Taylor, who was taking meetings in Ireland, adding a note to remind him that young Maria was about to arrive in Shanghai.

But the work of missions was not affected. Gertrude and Hudson were sent to Taiyuan, the capital of Shanxi. In a report to *China's Millions*, of which her father was the Editor, Gertrude described the rough nine-day journey which she and her brother took across north China from Baoding to Taiyuan, escorted by Dr. Ebenezer Edwards. Hudson in wadded clothes rode on a mule, Dr. Edwards went on a pony and Gertrude travelled with the luggage in a mule litter, covered over with matting. They reached Taiyuan on Boxing Day, 1885.

Gertrude proved to be a hard-working missionary in Shanxi. She was three years in Taiyuan, and travelled around on a donkey, witnessing largely to the peasant women who were opium addicts. Sometimes they came and stayed in her home. She wrote about several cases in *China's Millions*: 'The other day I went to an opium-smoking case, where the poor victim — a woman of about 30 — died. It was a dreadful sight, that dying woman, and her almost indifferent husband. Nothing so makes me realise the power of the Devil.'

In a subsequent issue she wrote: 'No. 3 of the Wang family came with a very bad mouth, and asked if she might stay a few days with us. She has been here ever since, and is much better. The day after our return from a journey one of the opium patients came. She has taken the drug for 13 years and in a large quantity. She looked such a wreck of humanity when she came.'

One case came from a different stratum of society. Like the rest of the population the Viceroys in Shanxi were also opium smokers. One day the daughter of one such Viceroy came for help. She stayed with Gertrude and became an active Christian.

Such cases Benjamin, as Editor both of *National Righteousness* and *China's Millions*, was able to use in his determined fight against the opium trade.

But in 1890 Gertrude Broomhall had to return to Britain, seriously broken in health. She had been carrying such a heavy burden, ministering to women opium addicts, that her delicate frame collapsed. Her friends in Taiyuan doubted that she would return, but they were to be proved wrong.

Seven years previously, in August 1883, when Gertrude was helping her father Benjamin in some office work in Pyrland Road, London, prior to departing for China, a tall lieutenant found his way to the CIM headquarters. He knocked at 6 Pyrland Road, and as he waited he could hear the playing of a familiar Sankey and Moody hymn. It brought back happy memories. He had heard the large congregation at The Dome, Brighton, singing it with gusto the night he had been converted. As he entered he saw Benjamin's petite daughter, Gertrude, playing at the piano. He resolved that night to himself that if ever there was to be a Mrs. Dixon Hoste, this fair-haired girl was she.

A year after this, in September 1884, Gertrude left for China in a small group of new missionaries, which was part of the 'Seventy'. Dixon left with the 'Cambridge Seven' in February 1885, five months later. Both had been designated to Shanxi. The two must have met soon after some of the 'Cambridge Seven' arrived, for *China's Millions* records that Gertrude was present at a conference in Taiyuan when Stanley Smith, Dixon Hoste and William Cassels, all recently arrived, addressed the missionaries. One wonders whether, in those days of strict social correctness in China, Dixon spoke to Gertrude and reminded her of their first meeting years before in Pyrland Road, London.

Dixon was in no hurry to propose marriage. In 1886 he joined Stanley Smith, also one of the 'Seven', and Pastor Hsi in a promising indigenous work which the Chinese pastor had started in southern Shanxi. There were groups of believers scattered over the Pingyang plain. Hoste was humble enough to be the junior worker under the other two — 'the cox of the boat'. They visited the churches in the villages and hamlets. At a single convention in Hong Kong in 1887 no less than 216 converts were baptized.

Smith moved on to commence work at Luan, and thereafter Hsi and Hoste worked together. Hoste was determined to see the work develop and grow under Chinese leadership, a strategy many years ahead of his time. He wore Chinese clothes, ate Chinese food and tried to get an insight into the Chinese mind. Hudson Taylor feared that Hoste might have gone too far, to the detriment of his health. It is interesting to mention that when Hoste had first applied to join the CIM Benjamin Broomhall had written to the vicar of his parish in the Isle of Wight for a reference as to his character and suitability. One of the observations which the Rev. W.T. Storrs had made was, 'He is not naturally fitted for missionary work, but I may be mistaken.' Time was to show how mistaken he was!

When Dixon Hoste declared his love to Gertrude, she was already preparing to return to Britain. She knew that if she were to agree to his proposal of marriage, the mission might lose both their services. So she declined, and Hoste in his loneliness shared the problem with the Lord in prayer.

Benjamin and Amelia were naturally pleased to see their eldest child again. Soon, in a more agreeable climate and more comfortable surroundings, Gertrude gradually recovered her health. But she wanted to continue serving the mission as she grew stronger, and so she took missionary meetings in both Britain and America, and her parents received favourable reports of her addresses.

After three years of absence from China, Gertrude bravely returned in 1893. Health had returned to her weary body and tired nerves. This time when Dixon proposed, she was ready to respond. At a conference of missionaries in Linfen in July 1894, there was general rejoicing when their engagement was announced. Then Dixon and Gertrude travelled with Hudson Taylor to Tianjin, where they were married on 6 September 1894.

When the newly-weds returned to Hongtong they had a royal welcome from the Chinese church. Dr. A.J. Broomhall records that in the church, there was a large blue banner on which were the characters in gold which said, 'With one heart serving the Lord'. They were given flowery furniture and bright curtains. Pastor Hsi presented the couple with a warm quilt covered with crimson silk, the bridal colour. All this shows the affection and esteem in which Hoste was held in his efforts to adapt to Chinese culture.

From now on Dixon Hoste took on increasing responsibility. His sensitive spirit and prayerful life fitted him for the difficult tasks which fell to him. First, in addition to his work in Hong Kong, he was made the Superintendent of the work in south-west Shanxi, with its twenty churches and four ordained pastors. Then he was transferred to be the Superintendent of nearby Hebei province. When the Boxer Rising came he was sent to Shanghai to help John Stevenson, who was carrying the heavy burden of the missionary casualties from the Rising. In 1901, with Hudson Taylor still recuperating in Switzerland, he was

Dixon and Gertrude Hoste.

made by his uncle-by-marriage, the Acting General Director of the mission, though only thirty-nine years of age. In the following year, three years before Hudson Taylor's death, Dixon was made the General Director.

This important position Hoste held for 33 years. In 1931 he launched a Forward Movement for the mission, appealing for 200 new recruits to advance into new spheres of work. He retired in 1935, aged seventy-four.

And what of Gertrude during these long years? Sadly, she experienced poor health again, and could do little to support her husband in his work, other than by prayer and loyalty. The writer recalls that whenever our family arrived at the Shanghai headquarters in Sinza Road, there were flowers and chocolates waiting for us in our rooms, and we visited 'Aunt Gertie' confined to her bed. Gertrude died in a mission home in Shanghai, 12 April 1944, over a year before the end of the Sino-Japanese War. Dixon died two years later, 11 May 1946, in the Mildmay Nursing Home, London.

We return now to Hudson Broomhall in Taiyuan. After a short period here with his sister Gertrude, he was sent to Hebei in 1887 to open up a station in Huolu. This was to be a receiving and forwarding station. Medicines and stores were sent from Shanghai by sea to Tianjin, and Huolu became a halfway house from there to Taiyuan. Thomas and Jessie Pigott (who were later martyred in the Boxer Rising), W.L. Elliston and Hudson Broomhall were the pioneers for CIM work in Hebei province. Under the leadership of Charles Green and Martin Griffiths, both of whom worked here for several decades in succession, Huolu became the centre of a strong circuit of churches, and in the 1920s Hudson Broomhall's son-in-law and daughter, Howard and Mary Cliff, were to work here.

Elliston died of sickness at Huolu, and the Pigotts returned to Shanxi, leaving the young missionary living in an inn on his own — a good opportunity to become fluent in the language and to get to know the local people. Hudson Broomhall wrote about his experiences at this time in an article in *China's Millions* entitled, 'Alone with God in a heathen city'.

He was not long in Huolu. In this brief time in Hebei he had shown his ability in administrative work, and this was to be the sphere of his labours for the rest of his life. After a year in Huolu, Hudson was sent to Chefoo (now Yantai) on the coast, and then to Dagutang in central China, overlooking the Poyang lake.

But to proceed with our story we must go back to Britain. Two years after Gertrude and Hudson Broomhall sailed for China, Benjamin Broomhall responded to a knock at the mission's front door. Standing before him was a cultured and well-dressed lady in a quaint bonnet. To Benjamin she looked too genteel and sheltered for the harsh life in inland China. Once in his study she told how she had been converted at the Sankey and Moody meetings in Brighton and felt called to serve God in China. 'But how will you manage the rough conditions of missionary life there?', Benjamin asked. The young lady replied firmly, 'God has called me, I must go'. Alice Miles was to marry Hudson Broomhall and become the General Secretary's daughter-in-law.

Alice went to China on 7 April 1887 in a batch of new missionaries who were part of the 'Hundred', arriving in Shanghai on 21 May 1887, after a voyage of six weeks. After attending the Language School at Yangzhou she was sent to Daning in western Shanxi. Alice and her colleague, Mary Scott, threw themselves into the work. Walking or riding on donkeys, they visited the small villages, which had been depleted by the recent famine. In one village where there had been 70 families there were now only 23, of whom 10 were Christians. It was truly front-line evangelism, and the missionaries were encouraged to attack and eradicate such evils as opium smoking, the binding of baby girls' feet, idol worship and concubinage.

Alice exuded happiness wherever she went, both among the missionaries and the peasant people. On 8 April 1889 she wrote: 'I really think that Taning [Daning] and its district must be the happiest vineyard in the whole length and breadth of China. The people love us and we love them.'

Was this not a reflection of her own capacity to love and be loved?

A month later she wrote of the baptism of seven candidates. The little gospel hall was crowded with visitors as Pastor Chu preached against wine drinking, tobacco smoking and foot-binding. After the service one woman smashed her pipe, and several mothers promised in future not to bind their daughters' feet. Their work was confrontational, but Mary Scott and Alice Miles seemed to get away with it through their tact and gentleness. Alice's reports speak of clay images being destroyed, paper images being burned, idol shrines being broken down and opium pipes being thrown into a bonfire. But it is clear that the people did not merely abandon certain bad habits, but came to a saving faith in Christ. These two single ladies were bravely facing the very powers of evil in western Shanxi.

While Alice was working faithfully in Daning, Hudson Broomhall had been for part of this period serving in Taiyuan at the centre of the province. Hudson had been a lonely bachelor missionary for six years. The best time for missionary romances was the regular conferences held in the capital. It must have been at one such gathering that Hudson Broomhall met Alice Miles. On 14 May 1890 they were married at Holy Trinity Cathedral in Shanghai.

The newly-married couple continued to work in Taiyuan for a further two years. After their furlough with baby Gershom, their first child, who had been given an apt name meaning 'a stranger in a strange land', Hudson Broomhall was appointed local secretary in Hankou, now part of Wuhan, in central China. It was here that my mother, Mary, and her sister Marjory were born.

They went from Hankou to Jiujiang in Jiangxi and to nearby Lushan (formerly Guling). Kathleen was born at Lushan, the first foreign baby to be born there. When the Boxer Rising broke out, Hudson and Alice Broomhall and their four children evacuated to Shanghai. After furlough in 1902 Hudson became

Hudson Broomhall and Alice Miles after their wedding on 14 May 1890 at the Holy Trinity Cathedral, Shanghai.

the local secretary at Chongqing, up the Yanzi river and in Sichuan province. Journeys between Shanghai and Chongqing in those days were extremely dangerous. Alice Broomhall, in an article in the *China's Millions* of March 1908 described just part of such a journey. There were frequent rapids, shoals and whirlpools. They were wrecked so often that they lost count of the number of accidents which befell them. It took them six weeks just to travel from Yichang to Wanxian, a distance of 150 nautical miles.

It was in 1918 that Hudson Broomhall took on the task which was to be his life-work. First he became the Assistant Treasurer of the CIM, and within a year became the Treasurer. This entailed moving to Shanghai. At first he worked at the mission premises in Wusong Road. By 1930 this property was proving quite inadequate for the expanding mission. Hudson's business acumen came to the fore. After speaking to estate agents he discovered that he could sell the Wusong Road property and build a more spacious and modern set of buildings at Sinza Road without further expenditure. Two large multi-storey buildings were erected, which included residences, offices, a hospital and meeting rooms.

Alice Broomhall found a fruitful sphere of service in Shanghai as Secretary of the Door of Hope — a Christian refuge for several hundred Chinese girls, aged from three to seventeen, rescued from the unholy traffic of buying and selling young girls for marriage. There were many tragic instances of these girls having been cruelly treated.

Hudson Broomhall died on 18 August 1934 of typhoid fever. The last 16 years of his life were spent as Treasurer of the mission. In a tribute to him in the *China's Millions* one missionary spoke of his competence as an accountant: 'Calculations, varying currencies, ever-changing rates of exchange and other complications had no terrors for him. He seemed in his element when surrounded by account books and immersed in figures, or busy with his calculating machine.'

When distributing the quarterly remittances to all the missionaries, he was always sensitive to the members' financial needs, for the remittance would vary according to the income received in that quarter. He always sent a brief letter with the advice, and the last one which he sent out read as follows:

My dear Friend,
With only a small remittance to send out, the first thought is: would that it were larger. It represents what the Lord has been good to send us during the quarter.

Alice retired to Chefoo, was interned there and in Weifang in the Sino-Japanese War, and died in Tunbridge Wells in 1953.

On 19 September 1888 twenty-one year old Edith, the third child of Benjamin and Amelia to join the CIM, sailed for China on the S.S. *Ravenna* with a group of other new missionaries. It was an exceptionally calm voyage, for the quartermaster told Edith that in the 16 years in which he had been at sea, he had never had a smoother passage. She was pleased to be at last on her way to the land which she had heard so much about throughout her childhood.

Upon her arrival in Shanghai, in writing to her father, the Editor of *China's Millions*, she expressed her feeling of excitement at actually being in China. She said that she was looking forward to Language School at Yangzhou, and even more so to being designated to her first station. She wrote, 'I am learning more and more that life is made up of so many little things, and these done to the glory of God are work for Him most truly.'

In 1889, after language study at Yangzhou, she was in Taiyuan, capital of Shanxi province, together with Gertrude and Hudson. Here she came up against the harsh reality of day to day missionary work, for the Chinese were not so eager to learn about Christianity as she had thought they would be. She wrote home about the 'coldness and indifference' of the Chinese Christians, and expressed her disappointment at the 'scanty welcome' which she and her sister Gertrude received in many homes. The missionaries were continuing to wage war against

Edith Broomhall as a young missionary in Shanxi.

opium smoking, the binding of girls' feet and idol worship, all habits which were deeply embedded in the Chinese way of life, and so the arrival at their homes of these representatives from the West were treated with a polite correctness which hid their instinctive animosity.

The women whom Gertrude and Edith visited were illiterate. The Christian instruction which was given was of the simplest. They were taught to hold out the five fingers of a hand, and recite:

> Thumb: There is only one true God,
> Forefinger: The true God loves us,
> Middle finger: The true God can forgive sins,
> Ring finger: The true God keeps us in peace,
> Little finger: The true God leads us at last to heaven.

In 1892 Edith moved with Gertrude to Daning, a small town on the western border of the province. Six years earlier a small congregation had been formed here through the labours of two of the 'Cambridge Seven' — Montagu Beauchamp and William Cassels. The two sisters worked hard to build up this young church, and they went on brief evangelistic tours in the country round about.

A typical such trip is described by Gertrude in the *China's Millions*. They formed a strange caravan. A Miss Stevens led the way on a mule cart, followed by Edith on a hired mule; then came Gertrude on a donkey, then a mule carrying their bedding and luggage, and lastly a donkey carrying their provisions. On a steep mountain road the mule carrying the luggage could not continue, and they had to rearrange the caravan. Edith helped solve the problem by insisting on walking. Such were the privations of being single women missionaries in inland China in the late nineteenth century.

Back in London, imagine the pleasant surprise which Benjamin and Amelia Broomhall had one day when a letter of appreciation and greetings from Pastor Zhang (pinyin spelling) arrived, which was duly translated:[1]

Specially addressed to:

The honoured and venerable Mr. and Mrs. Broomhall: Peace! Because God has answered prayer, and has caused us to receive the two dearly loved teachers Broomhall, all, including the writer, are delighted beyond measure.

But, fearing that in the venerable hearts of both of you there is much thought of them, may the God who comforts comfort you, and cause you in all things to receive happiness to the full. May the Lord constantly care for us, and assist us in causing His Word to be spread abroad in this place, taking to Himself the glory, and may He do the same in your midst. I invite you to look at II Thess. 2 v.13. We trust the Lord's great ability and great strength to help us, and to free us from sin's bonds, and cause many to be saved. I also invite you to look at II Cor. 1, vv. 20–22. May the grace of God and of the Lord Jesus Christ be constantly in the midst of your entire family, old and young, male and female.   Chang-chi-pen writes!

The work which Gertrude and Edith did in Daning included running evening meetings for the women and having meetings at noon for the children. According to Chinese custom at that time they could not preach to men, but when they treated the opium patients they inevitably came into touch with the male members of the community.

Unknown to Edith, while she was doing her evangelistic work at this time, the young man who was to be her husband was on the high seas en route to China. A young Scot, Gilbert Ritchie, had sailed from Britain on 5 January 1894 on the S.S. *Britannia*. He celebrated his twenty-second birthday on the way to Shanghai. He was only a few months at the Language School for Men at Anqing, where he found the language initially very difficult to learn.

He had come to China as 'the Glasgow YMCA missionary'. To his home YMCA he wrote from Anqing on the culture shock he was experiencing as a new arrival:[2]

> In the house opposite there was a death. In the evening two Buddhist priests arrived, and in a short time they came out carrying a paper house, horse and basket of money; also a basket of

provisions, to all of which they set fire. While they were burning they stood round beating drums and sending off crackers. The next night the priests returned, and began beating the drums again. They only beat them for a few minutes, then stopped, and the people in the house began wailing. This lasted for a few minutes, then the drums were beaten again. ... The house, horse money and provisions burned are for the use of the departed spirit in the other world, while the noise of the drums and the crackers is supposed to frighten the evil spirits away.

Gilbert Ritchie was designated to work under Dixon Hoste at Hongtong. On account of the Sino-Japanese War he had to travel by a circuitous route and took ten weeks to get there, arriving on 31 December 1894. He was always thankful that at his first station he had the privilege of working with Dixon and Gertrude Hoste. He later recalled, 'No young missionary could have chosen more ideal senior missionaries than the Hostes, nor could have had a better beginning to his missionary life.'

Dixon Hoste had been working for nine years in close association with Hsi Sheng Mo (a name meaning 'overcomer of demons'), a Chinese scholar and former opium addict. Together they had built up an extensive work in Shanxi, which included the running of opium clinics for the many addicts there.

Gilbert later wrote, 'It was while labouring with Mr. and Mrs. Hoste that I met my future wife, Miss Edith Broomhall, a sister of Mrs. Hoste and a niece of Hudson Taylor. She had been in China five years longer than I, and with her longer experience was able to give me, right from the beginning of our united lives, invaluable help.' Gilbert and Edith were married on 1 August 1896.

Pastor Hsi had died six months previously, and he had requested the young couple to open up work in the walled city of Yoyang, which lay as a jewel in the western mountains of Shanxi. Their Chinese helper was a converted Buddhist priest, who four years later in the Boxer Rising, was to be martyred. From Yoyang they extended the work to Qinyuen 'where,' Gilbert recorded, 'I had the joy of baptising my first convert'.

In 1897 and 1898 a son and a daughter were born — Alex and Anna. Furlough was long overdue. Edith had been in China 11 years without a break. As they prepared to depart they were aware of tensions in the villages and apprehension among the missionaries. On 13 December 1899 the Ritchie family arrived in Britain on the N.G.L. *Bayern*. Gilbert recalled, 'Alas, only a very few of my beloved fellow-missionaries in the province of Shansi escaped the blood-stained hands of the Boxers.'

On 9 July 1900 there was the 'Taiyuan Massacre' when, in one day, 35 Protestant missionaries, 12 Catholic priests and nuns and 30 Chinese were beheaded. Throughout China 135 adult missionaries and 53 missionaries' children were killed in the Boxer Rising. Of these numbers 113 adults and 46 children were killed in Shanxi province. In this disaster the CIM lost more missionaries than any other mission. The two young missionaries who took over the Ritchies' work at Yoyang, David Barratt and Alfred Woodroffe, fled to the hills from the Boxers, and died from their privations.

Gilbert went on to say, 'The way did not open up for our return to China, and I resumed my former occupation as a commercial traveller.' He never lost his interest in the work in China, and as a lay preacher constantly referred to this cause. Of Gilbert's six children, Edith became a missionary in Brazil and Anna a missionary in China, the land of her birth. Three children of another child, Alex, went into Christian work. Gilbert and Walter, at the time of writing, are serving as ministers of the Gospel in Scotland, while Carol, married to Angus McNeill, did medical missionary work in Zaire, and is now working with Angus in Thailand.

In 1887, at twenty-one years of age, Marshall commenced classical studies at Cambridge at the same time as his cousin, Charles Edward Taylor, fourth son of Hudson Taylor. After graduating from Jesus College Marshall became engaged to Florence Corderoy, the daughter of his father's close friend, John Corderoy.

Soon after graduating he was accepted by the China Inland Mission, and on 2 October 1890 he sailed for China on the S.S. *Shannon*. The mission's Register of New Missionaries recorded him as being a student and engaged to be married. He went to the mission field intending to spend his life in China, but circumstances were to force him to serve God in a different way, for he was to be there only nine years.

After a year at Language School at Anqing, Marshall was 'designated' to Taiyuan, Shanxi, where Hudson and Edith were already working. At this time there were epidemics and deaths from disease. When Hudson fell ill with typhus, Marshall himself contracted the disease through caring for his brother. For a time, Hudson, Edith and Marshall were unable to do their work. But, as already stated, all recovered.

From Taiyuan Marshall was transferred to Hongtong to work with Dixon Hoste, recently married to his sister Gertrude. Also at the station was Gilbert Ritchie, later to marry Edith.

It was four long years after his departure from England that Marshall's fiancee, Florence Corderoy, followed him, sailing for China in 1894. Mission regulations required that they could not marry until both had served for two years on the field.

When in 1896 Dixon Hoste was appointed Acting General Director of the CIM and moved with Gertrude to Shanghai, Marshall took charge of the important work at Hongtong. The church here had the largest membership of any church in Shanxi. The famous Pastor Hsi, 'bishop' of a group of churches in this area, had just died, and so Marshall had the difficult task of overseeing this 'diocese', which no longer had the services of Hsi and Hoste. These two pastors, a unique combination of Western missionary working under Chinese leadership, had worked together for ten years, and had planned an effective strategy together. In visiting the churches and preaching in them, Marshall learned much about Pastor Hsi's ministry, so much so that when his cousin by marriage, Geraldine Taylor (wife of Hudson Taylor's son, Howard) was preparing to write her classic two-volumed work on Hsi Sheng Mo [Xi Sheng mo], he was able to supply her with invaluable information.

**Marshall Broomhall and his fiancee, Florence Corderoy,
taken in Shanxi**

In a report in *China's Millions* in 1897 Marshall Broomhall described the new work in and around Hongtong which had fallen on his shoulders. The 'diocese' was forty miles north and south by seventy miles east and west. The total membership was 490, of whom 374 were male and 116 were female members. [Today in China the women exceed the men by far!]. There were 17 village churches, which had meetings every evening 7 days a week and 14 opium refuges which had been opened in earlier years by Pastor Hsi. To supervise this work there was a native pastor, three elders and seventeen deacons, and all this was self-supporting. There were also four schools subsidized by the mission. This was surely a model work with little input in personnel and money from the CIM.

The work was clearly growing, for a few months later Marshall reported that there were 72 new members, more than a 100 in the opium refuges had given up opium smoking, and two new chapels. In his final report in 1899 there were 33 new members (who had served a year's probation), more than 80 applicants for baptism, whilst 25 members had been suspended from receiving the Lord's Supper because of their opium growing, and three members had been struck off the roll, having lapsed back into idolatry.

On 17 March 1897 Marshall had married Florence. But two years later Florence's poor health necessitated their leaving for Britain, unable to return. Marshall had done three years of fruitful work in this fast-growing indigenous work around Hongtong. Having to leave this 'diocese' at such a time must have been a source of disappointment to him, but the Lord had other work in store for him, for which he was admirably suited. Their two daughters, Honor Irene and Dorothea, were born in Britain in 1901 and 1905.

In 1900 Marshall was appointed Editorial Secretary of the mission. Just five years after his father Benjamin had retired from the Editorship of the *China's Millions*, Marshall took over this important post. In his nine years in China he had learned the language and experienced the harsh conditions of missionary life. Without this knowledge he could not have carried out his new task so effectively. He revisited China and kept abreast of the mission's progress there. After the Revolution in 1911 and 1912 Marshall Broomhall visited China extensively to obtain firsthand knowledge of the new conditions there. He also gave preliminary lessons in Chinese to the missionary candidates in London as a preparation for their further studies on arrival in China.

In the 36 years which followed, Marshall produced over 20 books, an average of more than one new book every two years. These are listed in Appendix 1. Of these, three were general books on China, seven were biographies, two were on the Boxer Rising and eight on Hudson Taylor and the CIM. Of the three general books on China which Marshall Broomhall wrote, one was a mission survey on the Chinese Empire, one on Islam in China, and the third on the Bible in China. The former two books were originally written by Marshall at the request of the British government. They were read and studied by Catholic and Protestant missionaries throughout China. Of the seven biographies which he wrote, five were on CIM missionaries, one on Robert Morrison of the London Missionary Society and one on Marshall Feng, the 'Christian General' in Henan.

The books on Hudson Taylor and the work of the CIM were widely read, and served to publicise the mission very effectively. In 1929 Marshall published a new treatment of Hudson Taylor's life, called *Hudson Taylor, the Man who Believed God*. It went through no less than 23 reprints, and over 80,000 copies were sold. Applicants for the mission often referred to one or other of these books as having been used by God to challenge them about going to China. Also, in the monthly issue of *China's Millions* he wrote regular articles and book reviews.

Marshall took an important part in the well known Edinburgh Missionary Conference of 1910. He was a member of the commission on 'Carrying the Gospel to all the Non-Christian World', and constant reference was made to his widely read and important work *The Chinese Empire — a General and Missionary Survey*, and to the statistics in it.

Marshall lost the sight of one eye, but this did not deter him from keeping to his writing and editorial programme. In 1927 he retired from his position as Editor after 27 years, due to persistent insomnia. He died in 1937.

—————————

When the Boxer Rising came in 1900 all the Broomhalls had left Shanxi, the centre of the killings. Dixon and Gertrude Hoste were now at Shanghai, where Dixon helped John Stevenson to handle the correspondence and personnel side of the tragic event. Blow after blow fell on the mission as news came from the interior of further names of workers who had been trapped by the 'patriotic volunteers' and done to death. Sixty-eight year old Hudson Taylor, convalescing with Jennie in Switzerland, realised that he could not give the mission the leadership needed at this time. He cabled to Shanghai that thirty-nine year old Dixon Hoste was to be the Acting General Director.

Hudson and Alice Broomhall and their four small children were in Lushan (Guling), where Hudson was the local secretary for the mission, when the Rising broke out in north China. They evacuated to Shanghai. Marshall and Florence Broomhall were in London when the Boxer Rising began. Marshall was taking up his work as Editorial Secretary. Gilbert and Edith Ritchie had only recently returned to Scotland. The parents, Benjamin and Amelia, were now five years into retirement. Though they knew that all their children were safe from the Boxers, they wept as they heard that missionaries whom they had trained and sent out had been killed.

Alvyn Austin has shown that during the period in which the Broomhalls served in Shanxi, a Taylor-Broomhall dynasty was taking shape in the CIM. Dixon Hoste, Hudson Taylor's nephew by marriage, was to become the General Director; Marshall Broomhall was the Editorial Secretary of *China's Millions* and of the mission's publications; Hudson Taylor's medical son, Howard, became the Superintendent of Henan province, and later with his wife Geraldine travelled extensively researching as the founder's official biographers. Hudson Broomhall became the mission's Treasurer in Shanghai; J.J. Coulthard, married to

Maria, was for a time his father-in-law's personal secretary, and later served on the China Council. Benjamin and Amelia Broomhall, having served the mission for 20 years at the London headquarters, had gone into well-earned retirement.

Notes

1. *China's Millions* Aug. 1894, p. 141.
2. *China's Millions* Sept. 1894, p. 160.

13

Rebuilding from the ashes

Mildred Cable once wrote, 'The year 1900 holds the same significance as does the Flood in Old Testament Chronology. All China mission history dates before or after 1900.'

The killings and destruction of the fanatical Boxers gave missionary work in China a severe setback. The martyrs had to be buried, the Chinese Christians who had lost property and belongings had to be assisted, churches and hospitals had to be rebuilt and the normal work of evangelism and service to the people had to be resumed.

The province most affected by the Rising was Shanxi, where 113 missionaries of various societies and 46 missionaries' children were slaughtered. Of all the stations in this province the worst affected was the capital city of Taiyuan, for in the 'Taiyuan Massacre' of 9 July 1900, 35 Protestants (including children), 12 Catholic priests and nuns and 30 Chinese Christians were beheaded one after the other in the governor's *yamen*. The Schofield Memorial Hospital in this city and the adjoining missionary houses were destroyed.

In addition to the heavy losses sustained by the CIM in Shanxi as a whole, the BMS lost its entire staff of workers in the province, and all the missionaries of the small Shouyang Mission were killed except for Dr. Ebenezer Edwards and his wife, who were on furlough in Britain. Edwards said in later years, 'God did not count me worthy to die for Him in 1900.' The normal work of missions was interrupted for five years.

Dr. H.R. Williamson states:

> This grim story of Manchu imperial folly, as well as the treachery and cruelty on the part of many Manchu officials, is relieved not only by many glorious instances of Christian steadfastness and martyrdom, but by the conspicuous courage of other Manchu and Chinese officials, who befriended and protected large numbers of foreign missionaries and Chinese Christians in their various domains.

Among those who were shocked and challenged by the news of the suffering and destruction of the Boxer Rising was young Dr. Benjamin Broomhall, the tenth child of Benjamin and Amelia. Following his education at the City of London School, he was working and studying at the London Hospital in Mile End, where he would qualify as a Fellow of the Royal College of Surgeons and Licentiate of the Royal College of Physicians. His parents had been five years in retirement when the Rising took place, and were living in Pyrland Road, where the telegrams from China were being regularly received. The news of dozens of CIM missionaries being killed by the Boxers came as a shock to them, for many of these workers had been interviewed, selected and prepared for the mission field by them.

At the time of the Boxer massacres, Benjamin's uncle, Hudson Taylor, was convalescing in Davos, Switzerland. The CIM had lost 58 missionaries and 21 children. The tragic news of these killings had reached him in a succession of telegrams from China. Jennie had tried to stagger the bad news in order to protect her husband, who was already suffering from mental and physical exhaustion. Bowled over from the heavy losses of workers, Hudson could only say, 'I cannot read, I cannot think; I cannot even pray, but I can trust.'

In September 1900 when news of the deaths of missionaries in China was still arriving, Hudson's sister Amelia and her son Benjamin came to stay with the Taylors at Chamonix in Switzerland, and joined with them in walking and climbing. Dr. A.J. Broomhall records that his father, Dr. Benjamin Broomhall,

Dr. Benjamin Broomhall (Jun.), MRCS, LRCP, **who served in hospitals in Taiyuan and Xian.**

'borrowed Hudson Taylor's well worn ice-axe to visit a glacier with a guide'. As the young doctor listened to his uncle speak of the heavy losses of missionary workers in China as a result of the Boxer Rising, which was still proceeding, he must have been deeply moved. This became a 'Macedonian call' to help fill the gap in personnel.

_____

On 3 September 1903, 28 year old Benjamin sailed for China, the fifth of Benjamin and Amelia's children to take this step. Benjamin Jun. went out, not under the auspices of the CIM, but to serve the Shouyang mission as an independent worker, and with the financial support of a trust administered by Lord Rochdale and his family, who were members of the West Street Baptist Church, Rochdale. In the 'Taiyuan Massacre' the Shouyang mission had lost Mr. and Mrs. Thomas Pigott and their son Wellesley, Dr. and Mrs. A.E. Lovitt and child, leaving only one pair of missionary workers — Dr. and Mrs. Edwards. Also, many church members had been martyred. The Schofield Memorial Hospital and the homes of the missionaries had all been destroyed.

When Benjamin arrived in Taiyuan the evangelistic and medical work in the city had not yet been resumed. Church services had been recommenced, but there was much rebuilding to be done. The church was in disarray and everything had to be reorganised. In 1902 Dr. Edwards had handed over the work and properties of the small mission to the BMS.

Benjamin found Taiyuan to be a city of many memorials to the local martyrs. Stone tablets bearing the names of all who had died on 9 July 1900 were standing on the sites of their imprisonment and death. Two miles outside the east gate of the city there was the Martyrs' Memorial Cemetery, where the graves of missionaries and Chinese Christians lay in peaceful and beautiful surroundings.

His fiancee, Marion Aldwinckle, followed him soon afterwards to China, and they were married on 28 February 1905. Benjamin was now thirty and his bride twenty-three. Marion had qualified as dispenser with the Apothecaries' Hall and received her training at the Mildmay Hospital in Bethnal Green, London. She was to enter into the medical work of her husband with spiritual zeal and loyal support.

Ebenezer Edwards and Benjamin formed an effective team, and worked hard in rebuilding the new men's and women's hospitals. To the surprise of Edwards, Benjamin proved to be a very practical man, for he carried a large share of the programme of rebuilding and had an aptitude for this kind of work. In 1912 he supervised the building of the Nurses' Home, and in 1915 he installed a hot and cold water system in the hospital, and built isolation wards for the men's and women's hospitals. Edwards reported to the BMS, 'Dr. Broomhall is an ideal medical worker. He is not only a good surgeon, but can put up buildings, mend a clock or organ when almost past repair, keep the pumps in order, remodel the heating apparatus for the hospitals when necessary, and at the same time is very keen on winning the patients and others for Christ.'

As early as 1910, when Benjamin had only been working for seven years in Taiyuan, a report in the *Missionary Herald* spoke appreciatively of his work. It said, 'Drs Broomhall and Lewis have made a great reputation for themselves, and their names of Hai and Lu will doubtless be lisped pleasantly by the babes and sucklings of many successive generations.' In the same issue it was reported that 'the Prince Regent of China has bestowed the Star of the Double Dragon on the Reverends Arthur Sowerby and Evan Morgan, and on Doctors E.H. Edwards and B.C. Broomhall.'

As with all missionary work in China at that time, the work of Benjamin and Marion was interrupted by the turbulence of the country's history. The change-over in China from a monarchical regime of over 2,000 years to a republican form of government took place in 1911 and 1912 amid revolution and civil war. Most of the BMS missionaries evacuated to the coast, but Benjamin remained in Taiyuan to work with the Red Cross, helping with the wounded of whatever political conviction. With the formation of the Republic, Yuan Xishan became the 'model governor' of Shanxi, and brought in a period of peace and prosperity to the province which had been through the sufferings of famine and widespread opium addiction.

In 1916 the Broomhalls went on furlough, and stayed longer than planned as Benjamin served as a medical officer in the First World War. They returned to their work in China as soon as conditions permitted. In 1921 they were transferred to Xian in the province of Shaanxi, to the west of Shanxi, to work at the Jenkins — Robertson Hospital. A year after their arrival an explosion at an ammunition dump caused serious damage to the hospital building, and once again Benjamin's expertise in building and repair work was put to good use.

Funds were needed to carry out this repair programme. Benjamin wrote to the *Missionary Herald* about an encouraging incident. A Mr. Lu came to his house and expressed his sympathy and concern about the damage to the hospital, and gave him a cheque of $50. He went on to say that a year previously his wife was a patient in the hospital. She had not only been cured of her illness, but had been converted and baptized. While in hospital she saw an unwanted baby girl in a neighbouring ward, and arranged to adopt her. He in turn had been converted and baptized. This gift was an expression of his gratitude for the work done by the mission. Incidents such as these bring encouragement in the busy life of a missionary.

Marion, in addition to helping in the practical running of the hospital, loved to go from bed to bed and speak of Christ to the patients. In an article she wrote Marion revealed the underlying motive in her work. She said that she often looked at the crowds of men and women sitting in their respective waiting-halls. She looked past their misery and ignorance, and thought of what these people could become through the work of the Gospel and through education. She wrote, 'This is the hope that makes the work joyful. This is the stimulus which makes all service glad.'

But political upheaval was never far from the surface. In the late 1920s there was both the development of a strong anti-Christian movement in China and also bitter fighting between Communist and Guomindang troops. The Jenkins — Robertson

Hospital in Xian served hundreds of wounded soldiers of both rival factions. In 1926 Xian itself was besieged for nine months, and the missionaries had to evacuate to the coast. But Benjamin and the Rev. E.L. Phillips felt it their duty to accept the personal risk, and the 'Christian General', Feng Yuxian, urged them to stay. However, the dangers increased and these two workers also had to make their way to the coast. The missionaries returned in 1928. While Benjamin Broomhall was in Xian he supervised the installing of an X-ray plant, a novel innovation for those days, as well as of an artesian well. Both these tasks required considerable skill and expertise on his part.

In 1929 the Broomhalls were transferred back to the hospital in Taiyuan. Benjamin found himself serving, not only the large crowds at the hospital, but missionaries of all the societies, some of whom came long distances for medical help. His reputation had spread far and wide. Marion wrote in October, 1930, to Miss Bouser at the BMS office in London, 'This year we have already had 55 people to stay with us in the house — all missionaries — either passing through or ill, wishing to see the doctor. That makes my home duties heavy sometimes.' The writer's father, Howard Cliff, was one of these, and travelled from Hebei province. Writing to his mother in Torquay, he spoke appreciatively of the help and healing he had received from 'Uncle Ben'.

But the hearts of Benjamin and Marion were still in Xian. In the same letter Marion wrote, 'We left such great mountains of our hearts' love in Sian [Xian] that the move needed some adjustment ... [and more so because of] the continual pleading that we should come back from so many there. The overwhelming love of a few Shensi [Shaanxi] Chinese is such that they have come up to see us here.'

After nearly 30 years of loving and faithful service in China the Broomhalls returned to Britain, and prior to retirement, Benjamin had a medical practice in Dulwich, south London.

Let me close with a further quotation from the above-mentioned letter written in October, 1930, two years before retirement, 'This will be our last term in China. But if we can help to inspire our children with the joy of Christ, to see at least two or three of them come abroad, then our cup of joy will be very full.'

This desire has surely been fulfilled, for the two sons of the six children did go abroad to be involved in missionary work. Paul and his wife Rosalind served the Bible and Medical Missionary Fellowship (now Interserve) on its Council in Britain, and between 1950 and 1974 took five journeys to India and Nepal. Paul for many years served on the Council of the Overseas Missionary Fellowship, formerly the China Inland Mission, for which his grandparents Benjamin and Amelia had done so much.

Jim, the second son of Benjamin and Marion, a medical doctor, sailed for China under the China Inland Mission in 1938 and married Janet Churchill in 1942. Together they worked among the Nosu, a warlike tribe in south-west China, and established a church among them before the Communist revolution. From 1953 they worked for 11 years in the Philippines among the Mangyan people. Their pioneering and medical work has been well described in Jim Broomhall's books *Strong Tower* and *Strong Man's Prey*.

Jim's son-in-law and daughter, Dr. Ted and Joy Lankester, spent seven years in a community health project on the Indian Himalayan slopes under the Emmanuel Hospital Association and funded by TEAR Fund. At the time this book is being written they are active in the work of Medical Services International in south-west China.

Also at the time of my writing this chapter, MSI is planning the launching of hospital and community health programmes in Sichuan and Yunnan. This included a 'Broomhall Health Project' in the area of the Great Cold Mountains, where Jim and Janet once worked among a tribal group now called the Yi. Ted and Joy were active in the planning of this new work. And so the descendants of Benjamin continue to spread the Gospel.

14

When I lift my first finger ...

One of Benjamin Broomhall's last tasks before going into retirement was to plan and supervise the building of the Newington
Green offices of the mission. Dr. A.J. Broomhall quotes from the
mission's records at this time: 'Completed plans for offices,
meeting hall, thirty bedrooms and public rooms went before the
Council on May 2, 1893. Robert Scott and Benjamin agreed that
work should start ... Scott gave £500 and offered £2,000 on loan
towards it ... The loan was declined, but an offer of £3,000 by a
Miss Josephine Smith was accepted.'

He further states that the foundations of the new building
were laid in December 1893, and on 8 March 1894 the Newington
Green building was occupied. To Benjamin and Amelia this was
a fitting end to their 20 years of work there.

It is significant that the article in *China's Millions* entitled
'Retirement of Mr. Broomhall' ends with these words: 'Mr.
Broomhall would like all friends to know that he will still
continue to reside at No. 2 Pyrland Road as hitherto. The offices
of the Mission have now been removed to the new buildings at
Newington Green.'

In May 1894 Benjamin delivered his last Secretary's Report at
the mission's May meeting, and in April 1895 formally retired,
aged sixty-six. He was succeeded by Walter Sloan, a trained
company secretary, who in 1902 was to become the mission's
Home Director. The Broomhalls withdrew from the cause they
had served so long, with the work of the mission still growing

— a new headquarters just completed and occupied, and with the membership of the CIM standing at 630.

For Benjamin, going into retirement did not mean an end to his work. He had a firm conviction that there was still much for him to do for God. He wrote: 'I am prepared to throw up all other causes that may hinder my work for the overthrow of this dreadful trade [the opium trade], and with the help of one of my daughters will gladly labour on in hope, and in faith that God will be with us in the conflict ...'

For a further 16 years Benjamin Broomhall continued his work as Editor of the magazine of his Anti-Opium society on an honorary basis. This entailed reading the regular reports on the opium trade from India and China, supplying up to date information to members of Parliament to encourage them to keep up the pressure on the British government. Dr. James Maxwell frequently visited him to discuss the work and policy of the society.

Increasing deafness cut Benjamin off from social conversation and attendance at church. This deafness gave him increased opportunity to indulge in his only hobby — the reading of books. In the place of the services in church, which he could no longer hear, he received his spiritual food largely from Spurgeon's sermons.

Throughout his life he had purchased books regularly for his library. It was a family joke that he would smuggle newly acquired books past Amelia as though he was a naughty school boy. Marshall recalls: 'Every landing was full of bookcases, and, in consequence of the warning of an architect, one heavy bookcase had to be removed from his study, as its weight was endangering the floor.' Benjamin had a photographic mind, and knew the position of every book on his shelves, and, if looking for a quotation, knew exactly where on a page he would find it. Many passages he could quote by memory. He could skim rapidly through parliamentary reports to find what he needed, or scan a book quickly to absorb its essential contents.

In his childhood, Benjamin's father had discouraged him from reading novels, but as he grew older he became more tolerant and flexible. Lamb's *Tales from Shakespeare* he enjoyed in his later years, though not having been permitted to read it in his childhood. In his retirement he was able to enjoy novels and to share them with his children.

On 10 February 1909, Benjamin and Amelia celebrated their golden wedding anniversary. New carpets and furnishings were given them by family and friends, as well as gifts in money. Benjamin was now eighty and Amelia seventy-four, and both were enjoying good health. It is interesting to note that five days before his marriage in 1859, Benjamin wrote in a letter, 'I went this morning to see the consulting physician of the S — Insurance Company. He says he cannot pass me!' This was a judgment which time proved to be wrong.

Six months after the golden wedding anniversary, Benjamin paid a visit to the scenes of his boyhood in Bradley. James, his 61 year old brother, now living in Barnsley, took him around. Many of the spots which he visited he had not seen for 60 years. He wrote home:

> The country is lovely — fields and trees truly beautiful. ... The cottages of my boyhood have nearly all disappeared. I went into the old church yesterday. The gallery in which we used to have an array of bassoons, clarionets, and an enormous fiddle — and in which I was in the choir — have all been swept away, but the Church has been made very comfortable.

On Christmas Day, 1910 Amelia wrote in her journal, 'Is this our last Christmas on earth? We know not, but, thank God, fear of death has gone.' She was right. It was indeed to be their last Christmas together.

I have recounted in chapter 11 the wonderful sequence of events in which, just before Benjamin's passing, came the welcome news in *The Times* of 19 April 1911 summed up in a single sentence — 'This means the extinction of the opium traffic within, at the most, two years, or even earlier.' When Marshall read this to his father, the dying warrior gathered up his strength, and with a great effort said, 'A great victory! Thank

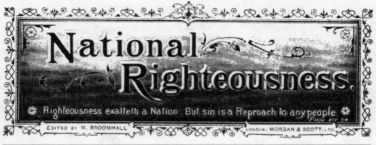

National Righteousness.

Righteousness exalteth a Nation : But sin is a Reproach to any people.
Prov. xiv 34

EDITED BY M. BROOMHALL

LONDON: MORGAN & SCOTT, LTD.

Vol. II. No. 26.   AUGUST 1911   Price One Penny.

Benjamin Broomhall at his desk in Pyrland Road, London.

The new offices of the China Inland Mission, Newington Green, London, opened in 1894.

God I have lived to see it!' Benjamin Broomhall had been spared to see the triumph of the cause which he had championed for many decades. It was in fact on 7 May 1913, after Benjamin's death, that the British Government announced, 'We are in the satisfactory position of saying that the traffic is dead.'

For days the patient was partially paralysed following a stroke, and the powers of articulate speech had virtually gone. As Amelia and members of the family waited on him, Benjamin wanted to express his gratitude, but speech was now very difficult. But with a special effort he did manage to say, 'When I lift my first finger, that means thank you.' He was determined to the end not to allow any act of kindness or thoughtfulness to go unacknowledged.

Benjamin Broomhall lingered on for more than a month after hearing the good news of the ending of the opium traffic. The regular lifting of his first finger told his family of his love and gratitude. He died aged eighty-one at his home in Pyrland Road. At the time of his passing, of the children who were missionaries, Hudson Broomhall, his son, was on the high seas hoping to see his father (he did not arrive in time to see him), Gertrude and Dixon Hoste were at the CIM home in Wusong Road, Shanghai; Benjamin was doing medical work in Taiyuan, Shanxi, while Marshall was at his father's bedside in London. Amelia survived Benjamin by seven years, and died on Easter Day in 1918.

Her family found on the flyleaf of her Bible a last message which she had written, knowing that her homecall was imminent:

> I am leaving, I am leaving
>   For the country of my King.
> Let not words of grief be spoken,
> Let not loving hearts be broken,
>   Rather let the joybells ring —
> For earth's wintry night is changing
>   Into everlasting spring.

Dr. F.B. Meyer said of Benjamin Broomhall:[1]

Not every soldier in the great campaign of Righteousness against the Wrongs of Time has the joy of hearing the note of victory ring out at the hour of his own sunset. But such was the happy lot of our beloved leader and friend. In another world Benjamin Broomhall has already been welcomed by our Lord as having had so stalwart a share in rolling away the stone from before the face of the grave where one fourth or one fifth of the race has been entombed.

Notes

1. B. Broomhall, *National Righteousness*, Aug. 1911, p. 6.

Postscript

When William Carey, the pioneer missionary, was preparing to go to India in 1793, one of his colleagues feared that the zeal with which they had formed the Baptist Missionary Society might falter, and the missionaries on the field be left uncared for. A leading minister in the group predicted that people would contribute adequately at first in a fit of enthusiasm, and then gradually lose interest.

Carey too, on the verge of departing to India, recognised this danger. He needed the Christians in England to pray for the work regularly, to give faithfully towards the support of the missionaries and maintain an administrative structure. So he drew four ministers into a room where they formed a binding covenant for life, namely that as he went forth in the society's name and that of their Master 'they should never cease till death to stand by him'.

At this time Andrew Fuller, one of this small group, saw the missionary project to India as similar to the digging of a deep unexplored mine. Carey was, so to speak, saying, 'I'll go down the mine if you will hold the rope.' All four who made this solemn pledge faithfully kept their promises of loyalty and support. Says S. Pearce Carey, 'Carey could not have been blessed with stauncher comrades.'

The first 'rope-holder' whom Hudson Taylor had was William Berger. This humble businessman helped Hudson Taylor in the formation and early development of the China Inland

Mission, corresponded with him as he travelled into the interior of China, gave regular donations from his limited means, and always had a warm welcome for Hudson Taylor and his family in his home in East Grinstead.

After Berger's retirement and resignation as co-founder and UK Director of the CIM, Benjamin and Amelia became the next 'rope-holders', though the nature of their work was different from that of William Berger. Hudson Taylor leaned heavily on his sister and brother-in-law through the difficult and exciting years from 1875 to 1895. He could never have carried out his rapidly growing work in the inland provinces of China without these two faithful 'holders of the ropes'.

The very nature of rope-holding is remaining in the background when important work is done. Benjamin liked to quote the words of Captain Robert Scott: 'It is the work done that counts, not the praise that follows.' He was reticent about putting his name to books which he had written. His first book, *The Truth about Opium Smoking*, quotes what other people had said about opium smoking. Though he himself had strong convictions, based on many years of studying the subject, he does not express his own opinion. Nor does his name appear on the cover.

Likewise his best seller, *The Evangelization of the World*, has only the title on the cover, not his name. His initials only appear after the Introduction. Although the vision of world evangelism expressed in the articles which make up this book helped to bring about the formation of the Student Volunteer Movement, with its motto 'The Evangelization of the World in this Generation' largely taken from the title of his book, the early founders seemed unaware of who had produced the book or chosen its title. That was undoubtedly how Benjamin wished it.

Benjamin Broomhall did the editorial work of the CIM's *China's Millions* for 20 years, yet throughout that period the words 'Edited by J. Hudson Taylor' always appeared under the title. Benjamin had selected the reports and articles received from China, laid out the magazine to include news about the missionaries and supervised its distribution, but avoided putting his name in a prominent place. His brother-in-law, usually in faraway China, had done the final check of the selections made and remained nominally the Editor. *China's Millions'* opening devotional article was usually written by Benjamin, but at the end of it there was either no name or just B.B. He was just the 'rope-holder'.

Benjamin had the joy of seeing the three worthy causes to which he gave his energies and devotion all reach fruition. The slavery trade in Africa and the USA, which was so strong when he first arrived in London, finally came to an end. The struggling China Inland Mission, which he joined in 1875 was small and much criticised, and when he retired in 1895 it had increased nearly twentyfold and was widely respected. On his deathbed he heard the welcome news that the opium trade would be finally phased out within a few years. But in none of these did his name become prominent.

Katy Barclay Wilkinson wrote a hymn, sung by earlier generations, which ends with the words:

> And may they forget the channel,
> Seeing only Him.

Doubtless that was Benjamin Broomhall's fervent wish — to do a task well, but not be noticed. Perhaps that is why so little has been written about a man who achieved so much for the Kingdom of God in the latter half of the nineteenth century, and why this book has had to be written a century later.

Bibliography

Austin, A. J., *The Land of Strangers* (Toronto, York University, 1996)

Binfield, Clyde, *George Williams and the Y.M.C.A.* (London, Heinemann, 1973)

Broomhall, A. J., *Hudson Taylor and China's Open Century*, 7 Volumes (London, Hodder & Stoughton, 1989)

Broomhall, Marshall, *The Jubilee Story of the China Inland Mission* (London, Morgan & Scott and CIM, 1915)

——*Heirs Together of the Grace of Life* (London, Morgan & Scott and CIM, 1918)

Cable, Mildred, and French, Francesca, *Something Happened* (London, Hodder & Stoughton, 1933)

Chadwick, Owen, *The Victorian Church* (London, SCM, 1987)

Collier, Richard, *The General Next to God* (London, Collins, 1965)

Coupland, Sir Reginald, *The British Anti-Slavery Movement* (Ilford, F. Cass, 1964)

Elliot-Binns, L. E., *Religion in the Victorian Era* (London, Lutterworth Press, 1936)

Gairdner, W. H. T., *The Edinburgh Conference of 1910* (Edinburgh, Oliphant, Anderson & Ferrier, 1910)

Greenslade, M. W. and Stuart, D. G., *A History of Staffordshire* (Chichester, Phillimore, 1984)

Heaton, Peter, *Staffordshire* (Aylesbury, Shire Publications, 1991)

Hodder, Edwin, *The Life of Sir George Williams* (London, Hodder & Stoughton, 1906)

Johnston, J., *The Centenary Conference of Protestant Missions in 1888* (London, James Nisbet, 1889)

Kirton, J. W., *True Nobility — Biography of the Earl of Shaftesbury* (London, Ward Lock, 1886)

Latourette, K. S., *A History of the Expansion of Christianity, 1800–1914* (London, Eyre & Spottiswoode, 1938)

Neill, Stephen, *A History of Christian Missions* (London, Penguin Books, 1964)

Pearce Carey, S., *William Carey* (London, Hodder & Stoughton, 1964)

Pollock, J. C., *The Cambridge Seven* (London, IVF, 1955)

——*Hudson Taylor and Maria* (London, Hodder & Stoughton, 1966)

Steer, Roger, *J. Hudson Taylor, A Man in Christ* (Singapore, OMF, 1990)

Taylor, Geraldine, *Hudson Taylor*, 2 Volumes (London, CIM and Religious Tract Society, 1918)

Taylor, J. H., *China, Its Spiritual Need and Claims* (London, CIM, 1865)

Temperley, Howard, *British Anti-slavery, 1833–1870* (London, Longman, 1972)

Thompson, Phyllis, *D.E. Hoste, a Prince with God* (London, CIM, 1947)

——*Each to Her Post* (London, Hodder & Stoughton and OMF, 1982)

Williamson, H. R., *British Baptists in China, 1845–1952* (London, Carey Kingsgate Press, 1957)

World Missionary Conference 1910, 9 Volumes (Edinburgh, Oliphant, Anderson & Ferrier 1911)

    China's Millions, (Magazine of the CIM)

    Evangelical Christendom (Magazine of the Evangelical Alliance, 2 March, 1885

    Letters of J. Hudson Taylor (In the OMF Archives)

    Missionary Herald (Magazine of the Baptist Missionary Society)

    Monthly Evangel (Magazine of the Findlay Memorial Tabernacle, St. George's Cross Glasgow)

    Minutes of the Bayswater Circuit of the Wesleyan Methodist Church.

    Notes on the Broomhall Family (Mrs. Alice Forrest)

    The Times (London, 21 May, 1911)

Books and Articles by Benjamin Broomhall

The Truth about Opium Smoking (London, Hodder & Stoughton, 1882)

The Evangelization of the World — a Record of Consecration and an Appeal (London, CIM, 1889)

Britain's Sin and Folly (London, Morgan & Scott, 1904)

Articles in *China's Millions*, Magazine of the CIM (Editor 1875–1895)

Articles in *National Righteousness*, Magazine of the Christian Union for the Severance of the Connection of the British Empire from the Opium Trade (Editor 1888–1911)

Booklet by Amelia Broomhall

Homely Hints to Young Mothers on the Training of Their Children (London, Morgan & Scott, undated)

Appendix I

Books by Marshall Broomhall

Martyred Missionaries of the China Inland Mission, with a Record of the Perils and Suffering of Some who Escaped (London, Morgan & Scott and CIM, 1901)

Last Letters and Further Records of Martyred Missionaries of the China Inland Mission (London, Morgan & Scott and CIM, 1901)

In Memoriam: Hudson Taylor's Legacy (London, Morgan & Scott and CIM, 1905)

Pioneer Work in Hunan by Adam Dorward and Other Missionaries of the China Inland Mission (London, Morgan & Scott and CIM, 1906)

The Chinese Empire, A General and Missionary Survey (London, Marshall, Morgan & Scott and CIM, 1907)

Faith and Facts, as Illustrated in the History of the China Inland Mission (London, Marshall, Morgan & Scott and CIM, 1909)

Islam in China (London, Marshall, Morgan & Scott and CIM, 1910)

The Jubilee Story of the China Inland Mission (London, Morgan & Scott and CIM, 1915)

Heirs Together of the Grace of Life — Benjamin Broomhall and Amelia Hudson Broomhall (London, Morgan & Scott and CIM, 1918)

John W. Stevenson, One of Christ's Stalwarts (London, Morgan & Scott and CIM, 1919)

F. W. Baller, A Master of the Pencil (London, CIM, 1923)

Marshall Feng: A Good Soldier of Jesus Christ (London, CIM and Religious Tract Society, 1923)

Robert Morrison, a Master Builder (London, Marshall, Morgan & Scott, 1924)

W.W. Cassells, First Bishop in Western China (London, CIM, 1926)

Hudson Taylor, the Man who believed God (London, CIM, 1929)

Archibald Orr Ewing, That Faithful and Wise Steward (London, CIM, 1930)

Hudson Taylor's Legacy, (London, Hodder & Stoughton, 1931)

Our Seal: The Witness of the China Inland Mission to the Faithfulness of God (London, CIM and Religious Tract Society, 1933)

The Bible in China (London, CIM and Religious Tract Society, 1934)

By Love Compelled, The Call of the China Inland Mission (London, Hodder & Stoughton, 1936)

Appendix II

Dates in the lives of Benjamin & Amelia Broomhall

Benjamin

1829 15 August — Born in Bradley
      Staffordshire
1844 May — moves to Barnsley
      (becomes draper's apprentice)
1847 23 January — Conversion
1854 Moves to London
1856 Begins correspondence with Amelia
1857 Engagement to Amelia

Amelia

1835 20 September — Born in
      Barnsley, Yorks

1849 Goes to school at Barton
1852 Moves to Dodworth Vicarage

1859 10 February — Marriage of Benjamin and Amelia
      Home at Westbourne Grove, Bayswater
1861 18 May — Birth of Gertrude
1862 31 August — Birth of Hudson
1863 22 November — Birth of Emily
1865 4 April — Birth of Mary Louise
1865 25 June — Hudson's decision at Brighton
1866 26 May — Hudson and party leave on the *Lammermuir*
1866 17 July — Birth of Marshall
1867 23 October — Birth of Edith
1869 9 September — Birth of Alice
1871 Family moves to Godalming
1872 5 June — Birth of Noel
1873 17 August — Birth of Anne Marie
1875 16 March — Birth of Benjamin
1875 June — Family moves to 2 Pyrland Road, London
      Work with CIM
1878 Benjamin made General Secretary of CIM
1885 4 February — Meeting of Cambridge Seven, Exeter Hall
1888 June — Benjamin attends London Missionary Conference

1888   Sec. for Anti-Opium Society
1895   Retirement from CIM
1900   Boxer Rising in China
1903   1 January Hudson appoints Dixon Hoste as General Director
1905   Death of Hudson Taylor at Changsha
1910   September — Edinburgh Missionary Conference
1911   Benjamin dies after Anti-Opium Campaign succeeds
1918   31 March — Amelia dies